The Kathryn Kuhlman I Knew

Jimmie McDonald

Treasure House

An Imprint of

Destiny Image® Publishers, Inc.
P.O. Box 310
Shippensburg, PA 17257-0310

"For where your treasure is
there will your heart be also." Matthew 6:21

ISBN 1-56043-272-1

For Worldwide Distribution
Printed in the U.S.A.

Treasure House books are available through these fine distributors outside the United States:

Christian Growth, Inc.
Jalan Kilang-Timor, Singapore 0315

Omega Distributors
Ponsonby, Auckland, New Zealand

Rhema Ministries Trading
Randburg, Rep. of South Africa

Salvation Book Centre
Petaling, Jaya, Malaysia

Successful Christian Living
Capetown, Rep. of South Africa

Vine Christian Centre
Mid Glamorgan, Wales, United Kingdom

WA Buchanan Company
Geebung, Queensland, Australia

Word Alive
Niverville, Manitoba, Canada

This book and all other Destiny Image and Treasure House books are available at Christian bookstores everywhere. Call for a bookstore nearest you.
1-800-722-6774
Or reach us on the Internet:
http://www.reapernet.com

Dedication

To Marlene Smith McDonald,
my wife and prayer partner in ministry;

to my daughters,
Carolyn McDonald Washington
and Judith Gail McDonald;

and to my mother, Margaret Bolden.

Acknowledgments

Dan Wooding, who shepherded the book from the embryonic stages right down through the birth canal.

Benny Hinn, who constantly reminds the world that there was a Kathryn Kuhlman and who rekindled the flame of worldwide ministry in my life.

Gene Polino, whom the Holy Spirit used to plant the seed into my spirit about writing a book.

The Kathryn Kuhlman Foundation and Carol, who remained at the helm of the ministry. "Thanks for the ministry."

George and Wendy Parson, who gave vision to my writing.

Paul and Jan Crouch and the TBN television family, who through the playing of the old video of Kathryn Kuhlman reminded me of my supernatural "roots" in the healing ministry.

Reverend Douglas Taylor, my pastor, and Dr. Stephanie Tayolor, his wife, for their watchful care for both the physical and the spiritual.

Ralph Wilkerson, pastor of Melodyland, who said, "Jimmie, I believe you have a book inside of you."

Reverend Eugene T. Grove, Baltimore, Maryland, in memoriam.

Contents

Introduction

"Lady, what is your age?"

When the immigration official at Tel Aviv International Airport in Israel asked this question just after our long flight from New York, he did not realize that he was asking Kathryn Kuhlman to reveal a secret that even those close to her, like myself, did not know the answer to.

"Sir," she responded firmly, "I do not discuss my age with anyone."

The official eyed her quizzically.

"Well," the man replied, "if you are going to get through this airport, I have to know your age. It has to go on your form. You have filled out everything except your age."

I held my breath as I stood watching this great lady contemplate how to deal with the situation.

Suddenly a slight smile came on her face and she opened her purse and pulled out a pen. As the bemused officer watched, she asked for a piece of blank paper and then slowly wrote her age on it. Kathryn neatly folded it in half and handed it to the passport official.

"Remember," she told him, "I never *told* you my age."

The man then wrote her age on the entry form, stamped her passport, and waved her through. As she breezed toward customs where her luggage awaited her, I saw him scratch his head.

I found it hard not to chuckle, but I also realized that Kathryn Kuhlman had made a decision early in her life not to discuss her age with anyone. Despite the tremendously high profile she had with the American public, deep down she was an intensely private person who did this to guard that little part of herself that was hers alone.

Although she was completely simplistic in her faith in Jesus Christ and the power of the Holy Spirit, she was incredibly complex as a human being.

That's the Kathryn Kuhlman I knew and loved for 15 years as a dear sister, colleague, and friend. This is the woman that you will learn about in this book, which is my tribute to one of God's great saints of the twentieth century.

She was a true original!

Jimmie McDonald

Chapter One

At the "Shrine" With Kathryn

*A*S I STOOD in the darkened wings of the historic Shrine Auditorium that was built in 1925 in downtown Los Angeles, the dramatic figure of Kathryn Kuhlman swept past me, a fixed smile lighting up her face, and her chiffon gown fluttering behind her.

To the flourish of organ music and deafening applause, I was witnessing another of her grand entrances to meet her adoring public and the hordes of sick people who had come for their miracle healing. Many had been pushed by desperate relatives into this famous, 6,500-seater, landmark auditorium to see the "Miracle Lady."

I had already sung my rendition of "His Eye Is on the Sparrow," and I now prepared to watch from my privileged vantage spot on the wings, this woman that *Time* magazine once called a "veritable one-woman Shrine of Lourdes," as she began to speak in long, husky, drawn-out syllables.

"Hellooo," Kathryn crooned. "Can't you feel the presence of the Hooooooly Spiiirit?"

Cheers rang out, as hundreds sat waiting in breathless anticipation for *their* miracle to take place.

After a few minutes of her dramatic sermon, Kathryn suddenly stopped, closed her eyes, and said, "I believe that someone is being healed from an ulcer." She then pointed into the hushed audience and said, "You, yes, yooou. The lady over there in the thiiird row. Would you come up here. God *has* healed you!"

All eyes were now focused on the lady who rose up from her seat and literally bounded up the side steps to be with the lady with the flashing eyes and red hair.

I was witnessing yet another extraordinary service with this exceptional woman with whom I had been working for nearly ten years. As I stood there and observed the woman from the audience giving glory to God for her healing, I allowed my mind to drift back to the situation that had brought me to this period in my life.

In the Beginning

I had to pinch myself that I had already experienced so much in God's ministry. However, I realized at that moment that I could not have gotten off to a worse start in life. My unmarried mother was only 15 years of age when I was born on December 19, 1937, in Baltimore, the largest city in Maryland, and one of the nation's largest seaports.

My parents, David McDonald and Margaret Brown, had never married nor lived together, so I was raised by my elderly great-grandmother, Mary Julia Gray. She was in her late 80s, and my mother also lived with us. I was the first boy in four generations of my mother's family.

I have often said that if today's liberal abortion laws had existed then, I would not be here today, since my mother would probably have been advised to "get rid" of me by her friends. Yet, I know my great-grandmother would have tried to prevent that from happening as she was a God-fearing Christian.

Although I never really had a live-in relationship with my father, from time-to-time I would hear him sing because he was the lead soloist in a black Southern Gospel quartet.

My great-grandmother took me regularly to the John Wesley Methodist Church in South Baltimore, a predominately black area, and I particularly enjoyed the exciting music that dominated the worship at this church.

As a child, I had quite a good voice, so at an early age I began singing publicly both by myself and with the choir there. I can still remember how, at the age of eight, I sang my first public solo, "Just Tell Jesus." I had a high-pitched, choirboy voice, and I received deafening applause when I sat down.

The Most Important Moment of My Life

A few years later, when I was 16, I was attending a Bible camp as one of the few blacks there, when the most important moment of my life occurred. I had been "horsing around" with the other boys, throwing the girls in the swimming pool, when one of the counselors who had been observing my behavior came over to where I stood, tapped me on the shoulder, and said, "Jimmie, I need to talk to you!"

The burly man was built like a football player, so I decided not to argue with him.

After we found a quiet corner, he glared at me and said, "Jimmie, I've been watching you and I haven't been very impressed with your behavior. Do you know the Lord? Have you been saved?"

I took a deep breath and countered with, "I've been in church all my life."

"Jimmie, I didn't ask you that," he said, fixing me with a stern look. "I asked you if you had ever been saved."

I shook my head and replied, "No, sir, I haven't."

"Would you like to be born again and meet the Savior?"

As his eyes bored into mine, I knew at that moment that I needed to get right with God. So there on my knees in the Pinebrook Bible Camp in Strasbourg on August 23, 1954, at precisely 10:00 a.m., I prayed the "sinner's prayer" and handed my life over to Jesus Christ.

Blessed With a Gift

Eventually, my voice developed, and I was awarded a scholarship to study to become an opera singer at the prestigious Peabody Conservatory of Music, a private institution in Baltimore that had opened in 1868. My hero in those days was the great black actor and singer, Paul Robeson, whom I later had the privilege of meeting.

In those "separated" days in America, the only way for someone like me to escape the ghetto was either through music or sports. I went for music.

At Peabody, the only form of music I felt I could enter was the rarefied world of opera. However, I met another opera singer named Anton Marco who showed me that it was possible to use my kind of voice to sing Christian hymns and gospel songs.

Not long after that, my singing abilities came to the attention of the Billy Graham Evangelistic Association, and I was invited to start working as a choir director and soloist with their associate evangelists: Howard O. Jones, John Wesley White, Lane Adams, Ralph Bell, and Grady Wilson. I also had the privilege of singing for Billy Graham at some of his major crusades, in places as diverse as Tokyo, Japan; London, England; and Kansas City, Missouri. I sang the old hymns and shared the platform with George Beverly Shea, who was known as "America's beloved gospel singer."

Singing to enormous crowds in huge stadiums and halls made my hair stand on end with the excitement of each occasion. It was a long way from the South Baltimore ghetto where I had been raised. Tears welled up in my eyes each time Billy Graham gave the invitation for people to "get up out of their seats" and give their lives to Jesus Christ. Almost before he finished speaking, people by the thousands would begin to stream onto the floor and stand in front of the platform, as counselors came and stood beside them. The tears would roll down my face as I witnessed the miracle of the "new birth" in the lives of these inquirers.

Besides working with the Graham organization, I was also invited to sing for other American evangelists, including Rex Humbard who had become well-known through his television programs. Rex and his wife, Maude Aimee, were a traveling evangelistic family originally from Arkansas. Along with Dad and Mother Humbard, they had been preaching for many years.

Up until this time, I had never been involved with the Pentecostals, but Rex was looked upon as a cross-over person who was accepted by both Pentecostals and those from other evangelical groups. Rex Humbard used to have an all-night telecast that he did on New Year's Eve from his "Cathedral of Tomorrow" in Akron, Ohio, and I sang in it. I remember on one occasion working with Stewart Hamblen, who had been converted at Billy Graham's 1949 Los Angeles crusade and had gone on to write the song, "It Is No Secret What God Can Do." Also, Rex Humbard put on a special presentation to commemorate the 200th anniversary of the founding of the United States and I sang at that as well.

On another occasion, Humbard had been asked to participate with the Cleveland Philharmonic Orchestra for a special event. The leader of the orchestra had told him, "We want you to send someone from your church to sing with us."

In his office, Rex asked me, "Jimmie, you have a background in classical music. Will you go? I'll fly you there, pay your way, and give you an honorarium."

He explained that this would be an "excellent way to minister the gospel to a secular audience."

So, with much trepidation, I flew to Cleveland and sang "The Penetant," the story of the Prodigal Son, with this great orchestra.

As I came off stage, Rex's wife, Maude Aimee, pulled me to one side and said, "I would give anything for you to meet Kathryn Kuhlman."

I looked at her blankly, having never heard of this particular lady.

"Look, Jimmie, I've already told Kathryn how blest I have been by your ministry and she wants me to bring you over to meet her."

Maude Aimee explained that Kathryn Kuhlman had begun her ministry in the late 1940's and had reached millions of listeners through media and stage appearances with a simple gospel message, "Believe in Jesus and be saved."

Maude Aimee went on to say that Kathryn Kuhlman's meetings were full of "supernatural healings" and this was what many people who went to her meetings expected to see and experience for themselves.

"Kathryn is also pastoring a church in Youngstown, Ohio, and each Friday morning she holds a

Bible study at the First Presbyterian Church in Pittsburgh," Maude Aimee continued. "I'd like to take you to one of them. But I warn you that it will be a long service, beginning at 9:30 a.m. and continuing until about 1:30 p.m."

I reluctantly agreed to go; so the next Friday I joined Rex and Maude Aimee in their car, as Rex drove from Akron to Pittsburgh for this service.

Meeting Kathryn Kuhlman

As I sat in the back seat of the car feeling trapped, Maude Aimee turned on the radio and told me, "Jimmie, I want you to listen to one of Kathryn's broadcasts. I think you will like it."

I really had no alternative, since I was held captive. I did not exactly know what to expect, though from the way Maude Aimee had described Kathryn Kuhlman, I figured that the voice of some kind of screaming woman would be coming through the speakers.

The broadcast began with a big choir introduction that I quite liked, though it did seem a little "over the top." Then Kathryn Kuhlman's voice echoed through the airwaves:

"Have you been waiting for me?" she asked in a powerful voice at exaggerated tones. "Then I would like to have a heart-to-heart talk with you."

I noticed that each word was carefully enunciated. She was so dramatic. It seemed like the way movie stars like Audrey Hepburn or Bette Davis would start a program. However, I later discovered that the reason she talked like this was because she had a speech impediment. As a child, she had stuttered badly, so the only way she could get around this difficulty was to carefully exaggerate the pronunciation of each word.

The more I listened, the more I got into her talk. I became captivated by the way she presented the message of Christ.

Besides appealing to the show business community, Kathryn also appealed to the hard-hat mill workers of Pittsburgh. Still, when we arrived at the church, I was expecting to meet a Hollywood-type person.

"Jimmie, don't expect any music this morning," said Maude Aimee. "Kathryn doesn't use a choir for her Friday services."

Rex and Maude Aimee ushered me into a back room at the church. As we walked in, Kathryn Kuhlman stood up and embraced us. "Welcoome!" she said.

I took a hard look at this unusual lady, and at first glance she did appear to be like what I considered the typical, eccentric, Hollywood movie star. Her chiffon dress and permed red hair gave her the appearance of someone who had just come off a sound stage at MGM studios. This Missouri-born woman, who had become the foremost woman evangelist of our century, was quite a sight to behold.

Then Maude Aimee said, "Kathryn, this is Jimmie McDonald, the singer I told you about."

Kathryn turned to look at me, and her eyes seemed to bore into my very soul, which made me extremely uncomfortable.

"I would like to hear him sing," she said. "Mr. McDonald, would you sing for us this morning?"

I nodded my head in the affirmative, but my tongue was tied!

The beautiful sanctuary was packed, and after the service began, Kathryn introduced me to the congregation. Then, with the accompaniment of a man on the piano, I sang "His Eye Is on the Sparrow." I sang from my heart to this mixed congregation of people from Roman Catholic, Greek Orthodox, Lutheran, and others from around the world, all forgetting their denominational ties.

Once I had completed the song, I turned to Kathryn and could see her eyes were alive with excitement.

"You *have* to be with me!" she gushed. "You have got to be part of *my* team."

So began my long association with Kathryn Kuhlman.

Initially, I had to deal with some uncomfortable theological problems that her ministry of "supernatural wonders" had placed before me. In those early days, I would squirm when she touched the foreheads of people and they "fell under the power," to be caught and eased to the ground by a "catcher."

It was all so different from a Billy Graham crusade. Was it of God or just pure emotionalism? That was the question I wrestled with.

Chapter Two

Two Different Worlds

*T*HE EARLY LIVES of Kathryn Kuhlman and Jimmie McDonald couldn't have been more converse. In fact, we came from two completely different worlds.

Kathryn first saw the light of day in the central Missouri farmlands. The late Jamie Buckingham, in his book *Daughter of Destiny,* described the area in this way:

> "When the winter whips across the prairies in a howling blue norther, driving snow and sleet before it like stinging, numbing nettles, they say the only thing between Concordia and the North Pole is a barbed wire fence—and even that's fallen down."[1]

The long, frigid winter had finally been chased away by the warming rays of the sun when Kathryn was born on May 9, 1907, five miles south of Concordia on a 160-acre farm in a small Lutheran community about 60 miles east of Kansas City. Her father was a tall, curly-haired farmer of German extraction named Joseph A. Kuhlman, and her mother was Emma Kuhlman, née Walkenhorst.

My background was not like this at all as a black person raised in the decaying streets of South Baltimore. As I mentioned before, I was born out of wedlock to my 15-year-old mother and was raised by my great-grandmother.

There was only one similarity between us as children: Kathryn was subjected to discipline from her mother, who felt that her husband was "far too soft" with this headstrong redhead. (Papa and young Kathryn idolized each other, and no one was prouder than Kathryn when he was elected mayor of Concordia.) My great-grandmother had experienced the same feelings about her rebellious young great-grandson and often took the leather belt to me.

Different Conversions

I first accepted the Lord into my heart at a summer camp, but Kathryn made the greatest decision of her life during a two-week revival meeting led by the Reverend Hummel, a Baptist evangelist, at the tiny Methodist church in Concordia.

On that life-changing Sunday morning, Kathryn was standing with her mother at the close of the service. As the minister gave the "invitation," Kathryn began to cry. She realized that she had been "touched by the Holy Spirit," and as Jamie Buckingham wrote in his book:

> "The sobbing was intense, so intense she began to shake. Kathryn dropped her hymn book into the rack in the back of the varnished pew in front of her and staggered out into the aisle. Her classmates, two rows in front of her, were startled and wide-eyed, as she ran down the aisle and collapsed into the front pew. Dropping her head into her hands, she sobbed so loudly, she could be heard all over the church."[2]

So there, in 1921, at the age of 14, Kathryn Kuhlman experienced the "new birth," and she knew that from that moment on she would never be the same.

On the "Sawdust Trail"

Kathryn got her initial experience of riding on what was called the "sawdust trail" with her older sister, Myrtle, who supported her evangelist husband, Everett B. Parrott, and traveled with him from town to town holding tent meetings. Because Myrtle was desperately unhappy with her marriage, she had asked Kathryn to go with her to Oregon for some meetings and be her companion. So in 1923, Kathryn joined her sister and Everett B. Parrott for several years of "whistle-stopping" from town to town with the "Parrott Tent Revival" team; at each place the preacher delivered in a loud voice the one message he knew, "Repent and be saved."

Eventually Kathryn split from the team and began her own services with the team's keyboard musician, Helen Gulliford. They billed themselves as "God's Girls" and held their first meeting in Pocatello, Idaho. These two attractive girls were soon pulling in the crowds.

In the early 1930's, Kathryn would stay late after the meetings to "pray through" the inquirers seeking salvation. It was during one of these "after meeting meetings" in Joliet, Illinois, that Kathryn had her first experience with the phenomenon of "singing in tongues."

Isabel, one of the women at the "afterglow," began singing in a language that Kathryn had never heard before. She said later, "It was so ethereal, so beautiful, that I felt the hair on my skin begin to rise." Isabel's mother said that her daughter couldn't usually carry a tune, and it was all she could do to refrain from jumping up and running around the room. Although the words and music sounded like they might be some ancient Greek or Phoenician chant, Kathryn knew their origin was not earthly.

This was the turning point in Kathryn Kuhlman's ministry, and it was not long until "signs and wonders" became a regular part of her meetings.

This phenomenon began to draw huge crowds of people who were looking for the reality of supernatural power in their lives.

The rest, as they say, is history, as this long-legged redhead ministered salvation and healing to millions of spiritually and physically sick people, both face to face and through her radio and television programs.

My Suspicions

I have to admit that when I first began to work with Kathryn Kuhlman, I was deeply suspicious of her and the "gifts of the Holy Spirit" that she "practiced" in her meetings.

The Billy Graham services I had attended were always focused on evangelism and not on signs and wonders. I had felt completely at ease with Mr. Graham because his crusades were more in line with the kind of Christianity that I had been brought up in by my dear great-grandmother.

In those early days of being part of Kathryn's team, I did not have a spiritual role model in the "deeper things of the Holy Spirit." There were few preachers then of the kind of modern-day preachers like Benny Hinn (with whom I now work), Jack Hayford, or Oral Roberts. Kathryn paved the way on television for people like Pat Robertson of CBN, Paul Crouch of TBN, or Jim Bakker of the *PTL Club.*

Curiosity and Confusion

"James, watch out for those religious cultists" was the advice I was given as a little boy raised in the ghetto by my deeply religious great-grandmother. I now believe that if it hadn't been for my great-grandmother's influence, I would have easily been caught up in one of these cults because I had such an interest in the supernatural.

Contributing to my confusion about signs and wonders, I got saved in a conservative group where the people believed that healing was "not for today." I had wanted to study God's Word in more depth, so I attended a Bible college. A teacher at this conservative Bible college told us students that "tongues and healing" were "dispensational" and were "not for today's Church."

Then I met Kathryn Kuhlman. Even during those first few months of singing at her larger-than-life "miracle crusades," I fought hard to deal with the kinds of things I was witnessing each night as people were being healed, getting out of their wheelchairs, and running across the stage to the wild applause of the audience.

While this was happening, I would stand on the stage, a few feet away from Kathryn Kuhlman, and see these extraordinary manifestations, and I would allow my mind to drift back to my childhood in Baltimore.

As a boy, I had been fascinated with the "supernatural" aspects of the cults that had sprung up in the black community of my home city. I compared these bizarre preachers with Kathryn and wondered if she too was a cult leader.

Someone once said, "The person with the experience is never at the mercy of the person with the argument." Yet, my only experience with the supernatural in those days was through these occultic groups, and because of this negative experience, I almost rejected Kathryn Kuhlman's ministry. (Later on in my Christian life, I was able to discover that satan often presents counterfeits of true ministry.)

Probably the most bizarre "healing" evangelist I ever came across in my childhood was "Sweet Daddy Grace," who had a group of black churches across America that was called "The House of Prayer."

At the tender age of eight, my fascination with Sweet Daddy Grace was not without its problems. In fact, it caused me a lot of physical pain.

Against the orders of my great-grandmother, I would sneak out to his exotic gatherings, even though I knew she would whip me with a leather belt when I returned home. Still, I thought the experience was worth the punishment because it was like entering a whole new realm that I had never seen before in my "conservative world."

A Frenzy

During that time Sweet Daddy Grace had become the talk of the black community, and I went to see him several times at the local House of Prayer.

At exactly 8:00 p.m., a ten-piece band would begin to whip the audience up into a four-hour frenzy before Sweet Daddy Grace would make his much-anticipated appearance.

About midnight, when the excitement had reached almost total hysteria, it was time for Sweet Daddy Grace to make his dramatic appearance. He always arrived in his long, sleek, black limousine, accompanied through the mean streets of South Baltimore by a motorcycle escort with sirens blaring and lights flashing.

I was very impressed with this because to a little boy who grew up in a city where blacks could not go to the same restaurants as whites, and were restricted as to where we could have our picnics in the park or where we could shop in the main department stores, this seemed particularly exciting. Sweet

Daddy Grace appeared to be saying that he was above "the white man's rule" of segregation.

This American version of apartheid meant that blacks had to shop in the basements of the stores, and were not even allowed into the downtown shops. Obviously, I was very impressed by a black man who had the power to ride through the city in a long black limo, escorted by white police, and go through red lights without being stopped or penalized.

When Sweet Daddy Grace arrived at the church, a long red carpet was rolled out before him so he could make his dramatic appearance. Sweet Daddy Grace then strutted like a preened peacock across the carpet to his carved wooden throne up on the platform.

His female disciples, who were clad in long white dresses and cotton stockings and wore no makeup, sang and danced in the aisles until Sweet Daddy Grace arrived. Then these "Angels" waited on him, fanning him and serving him water.

In those days, very few churches had air-conditioning, so in the stifling summer heat the perspiration flowed freely from all of us packed into the sanctuary like sardines.

When Sweet Daddy Grace sat down, the "Angels" would break out in what we would call today "praise and worship dancing."

Sweet Daddy Grace was a sight to behold. He was in his 70s and had long, gray, curly hair that drooped over his shoulders. He wore an expensive suit and had long fingernails that had grown five or six inches in length and were painted red, white, and blue. The crowd looked at him with adoring eyes.

Once Sweet Daddy Grace had taken his place on his throne, his burly black bodyguards surrounded him and glared into space. The scene was completely surreal.

Then, he clapped his hands, and the music began again; the people, including me, would get into "the Spirit" and dance in front of the pews or in the aisles. People would speak in tongues with interpretation, and after that, Sweet Daddy Grace once again clapped his hands and everyone formed a line. As they passed by him, he stood to his feet and touched them, and they fell on the floor. Then the ladies covered the "slain" people with white pieces of cloth.

The most frightening time for me came when the "offering" was taken up. Sweet Daddy Grace commanded that all the doors be locked so that people couldn't even go to the rest room. Like everyone else there, I was trapped, and I knew that once I eventually escaped, my great-grandmother would be waiting for me....

As Sweet Daddy Grace began to arrange for various lines of people who would give their "love offerings" of 15 or 20 dollars, a fortune in those days for a black person to part with, a trickle of fear went down my spine.

On my first visit, I began to panic as I searched my pockets. In a voice that was high and despairing, I turned to the person next to me and asked desperately, "Could you loan me a nickel? I've got to get out of this place and he won't unlock the door until we have all given something!"

There was a long, tantalizing moment of silence, as the sweat began to run into my eyes. Then his big, callused hand held out to me the silver coin I had requested. I clutched it with the fervor of a drowning boy catching a rope.

After the collection had been taken up in big trashcans, the money was carried out and the doors were unlocked.

Then came the period of "healing." Growths and goiters "disappeared." Crutches were thrown down on the floor as people walked. All over the walls of the church were canes, crutches, prostheses, and leg braces of people who had been "healed" and no longer needed them.

After nearly 90 minutes of this, Sweet Daddy Grace walked down the same red-carpeted aisle, and left in the same "blaze of glory" that he came in.

Even after he left, no one seemed to want to leave the building. Everyone was talking about what Sweet Daddy Grace had done for them.

For me, it was now time to face the music. As I walked along those echoing streets back to my home, I knew my rump would soon ache again. It would be a wowser, at least a ten on the Richter scale, as my great-grandmother gave me a series of seismological thuds.

Yet the exhilaration of these meetings were, for me, worth the whipping from my great-grandmother that I knew awaited me when I returned home in the early hours of the morning. Despite the warnings she gave me to "Stay away from that mess," I was so fascinated with Sweet Daddy Grace, and those like him, that no amount of punishment could keep me away from his meetings.

There were also other bizarre "healers" around, such as "Prophet Jones," "Father Divine," and "Prophet Cheery," who all practiced their weird ways in the halls and churches of South Baltimore. Many of them advertised on the radio and this would bring in huge crowds to their meetings.

The black radio stations carried advertisements for them that made wild and wonderful claims for each of these people. "They can see into your very soul and heal you from any illness" was the type of thing that I would hear on the radio in my house. (These were the days before the "psychic hot lines.")

I found out later that many of these men were homosexuals, and I asked myself, "How can so many people be deceived?" Yet, even as a child, I realized that there was a great hunger for the supernatural and that people would embrace anything that looked like it came from God, however counterfeit it might be.

Someone asked me one day, "If the religious cults were not of God, how could they do such supernatural things?" Basing my answer on Exodus 7:10-12, I replied, "God used Moses and Aaron to do some miracles in front of Pharoah. Aaron cast his rod down before Pharoah and it became a serpent. But Pharoah would not be outdone. He called for the sorcerers, the wise men, and the magicians (the psychics of his day). They cast their rods onto the ground and the rods became serpents, but Aaron's rod swallowed up their rods."

Sometimes we bring baggage into our spiritual experience. We form preconceived ideas or learn habits of worship that may not have any biblical foundations. The supernatural experience can be a dangerous weapon in the hands of the biblically untrained person. Hot, untrained emotion without the Bible produces fanaticism, and minds trained in the

Bible without the emotions of the heart produce a cold religious denomination. However, I have come to believe that the hot emotional experience combined with the trained biblical understanding produces a well-balanced experience.

The Bible calls us to be able to give a reason for what we feel and understand. It was through that kind of thought that I eventually looked at Kathryn Kuhlman and was able to accept her ministry.

Chapter Three

A Sense of the Dramatic?

SOME PEOPLE ACCUSED Kathryn Kuhlman of having a fine sense of the dramatic. In fact, some have said that all of her gatherings were "highly staged" and contained both planned and impromptu melodrama. I am not sure that I agree with them, but I do know that anything Kathryn Kuhlman did during her services only approached the amazingly dramatic incidents we find contained in Holy Writ.

Still, her services were something to behold. For instance, when she walked on stage with the music of the choir singing, "Nothing Is Impossible," she would allow the atmosphere to build and build. Then they would begin to sing "How Great Thou Art," and Kathryn would sweep across the stage with the frills and flurries of her dress adding to the drama, and it was a "great production."

I have heard some people criticize this, but in my own mind, I believe that Kathryn did what God has been doing for us from the beginning of time—using "great drama" to illustrate His message of love and reconciliation. Also, the Bible presents the prophetic use of music. As the Israelite forces would go into war, there would be music, and we also know that music will be used in the Second Coming of Jesus.

If we conclude that Kathryn's service was dramatic, then it was not unlike the dramatic way God did things. Almost everything God did had drama and production in it: At the creation of the world, God took a void of darkness and turned it into startling light; for Moses, God performed the great drama of parting the Red Sea; when Elijah was on Mount Carmel, God sent fire from Heaven.

But there was no greater drama than that which took place on the sacred hill of Calvary over 2,000 years ago. For at that history-changing moment, the sky turned dark and the earth shook as it belched forth all the venom it had been holding through the curse; for that which was vomited up was the phlegm of the pain of death.

The greatest drama in history was being played as Jesus died a terrible death on a cross to give a debased world heart-to-heart resuscitation that man would die no more.

Now that's what I call drama!

My own life experienced the heart-to-heart resurgence on August 23, 1954, when I felt the sorrow of my own sins and the joy after the confession of them.

Drama yes! It was an incredible moment for me. I thank God for the drama of the cross and the shed blood of Jesus that allows us to go back over time and see where we have gone wrong. And, as Grandmother used to say, "This how you got over it, Jimmie," meaning, this is how we made it through the difficult time.

Yes, Kathryn was dramatic, but certainly not as dramatic as that!

The Stambaugh Auditorium

Kathryn Kuhlman held her Sunday morning church services at the beautiful Stambaugh Auditorium, located in Youngstown in northeastern Ohio near the Pennsylvania border. This concert hall seated up to 3,000 people and had the kind of ambiance that Kathryn liked for her meetings.

Music played a vital role in all Kathryn's gatherings and her home church was no exception. Kathryn had a large choir, and she would pack the place for special musical events.

People would tell me, "Jimmie, wait until you see the morning service. It is amazing—something quite special!" Even though I had been told about them, I was not quite prepared for what took place until I witnessed it for myself.

Kathryn had invited me to sing at a communion service, and when I arrived, she greeted me in her usual effusive way and said how "glaaad" she was that I was there. "Jimmie, you will be a real blessing to all of us this morning," she had declared.

When I entered the auditorium, you could almost cut the electrically charged atmosphere with a knife. The nearly 400 male and female choir members were all smartly dressed in black and white and seated at the back of the stage behind the curtain. I stood in front of them, also hidden by the curtain, with a large black Bible in my hands. Suddenly, the buzz of conversation stopped as the curtain slowly began to open and the lights with their colored gels hit the choir, producing a kind of classic worship atmosphere.

As the choir began to sing the anthem, I felt like I was being lifted from my seat, like I was before the very throne of God in Heaven. I was reminded of the words from Isaiah 6:1,4 which say "...I saw also the Lord sitting upon a throne, high and lifted up, and His train filled the temple. ...and the house was filled with smoke." It certainly was dramatic! I realized that all of us there that morning were being lifted to a level that was totally different from one of Kathryn's crusade services.

One of the most moving parts of that Sunday morning gathering came when Kathryn turned to the choir and said, "Okay, choir, you may leave the platform." As the regular church singers left the stage, Kathryn called for a group of men who were seated all over the auditorium to "come and sing." They quickly rose up from their seats and made their way onto the stage.

After they had taken their places, Kathryn stood majestically in the middle of them, waving her hands with ill-controlled excitement, and said, "All right men, I want you just to sing it for me." As they began to raise their voices in praise to their Lord and Savior, Jesus Christ, tears began to course down Kathryn's cheeks. The more they sang, the more her body began to sway in what I call the "Kathryn Kuhlman movement." It was a tremendously moving scene.

When they had completed their first song, her voice rose an octave as she said, "Sing it again, men, because you know what you are singing about! You have all been delivered by this mighty power of the Holy Spirit and by the love of Jesus."

Their voices began to swell again, and I closely studied the faces of each of these men. As I did, they appeared to shine even more as I realized that all of them were voicing their personal story of how God had delivered them from a prison of hell. I discovered later that the men in this group were former alcoholics and drug addicts who had been delivered through Kathyrn Kuhlman's ministry.

A Prayer That Could Kill

After this unusual choir had completed their final song, I noticed a man standing quietly on the stage clasping a bunch of roses. His face was wreathed in smiles. He glanced towards me and then leaned over and said, "Hi, Jimmie!"

I slowly responded with a weak "Hello," but he realized from my quizzical look that I did not know who he was.

"I guess you don't remember me," he murmured.

Feeling embarrassed, I replied, "I'm sorry, sir, but I do not."

"That's all right," he continued. "I met you about a year ago at one of Kathryn's services."

It was then that I stopped him and snapped my fingers. "I do remember you," I said, as a smile crossed my face. "You were that man with a long unshaven beard and torn clothes, who wreaked from the smell of alcohol. You said your mother-in-law had brought you to the service because your wife and children had left you because you could not stop drinking."

He nodded. "And," I pressed on, "she had brought you to Kathryn Kuhlman as a last effort to get you to turn around."

My mind then flashed back to that extraordinary occasion. This formerly disheveled and broken man had stood on stage with Miss Kuhlman as she looked at him with piercing eyes and asked him, "What are you doing here and what do you want?"

Kathryn then paused as she saw the older woman standing with him. "And who is this lady with you?" she had asked.

The congregation was silent as he replied, "This is my mother-in-law. She has brought me here today because I am an alcoholic and I can't stop drinking."

Kathryn laughed and then said, "You have come to the right place." Then her face became serious. "Do you really want to stop drinking?" she asked him as he stood there shaking uncontrollably.

"Yes, ma'am," he said firmly.

Kathryn then began to pace back and forth across the stage as if she was getting a message from God. All of a sudden, she stopped and said, "All right! All right! All right!"

Kathryn then pointed her long, bony finger at the man and told him to repeat the following words after her:

"Dear Jesus."

He said the words after her.

"I need Your help! I can't do this on my own. If I take another drink, then You will make me sick unto death."

The man stopped when she said these words. Kathryn looked at him and then, in a thunder-like tone, said, "Young man, are you serious? Do you really mean business?"

My eyes moved from Kathryn to this quivering figure and it was then that I saw perspiration beading his furrowed brow. He began wringing his hands, and the silence seemed as if it was going to continue forever. We all realized that his very life depended on his answer.

The man finally took a deep breath and said, "Yes, Miss Kuhlman. I do mean business!"

Then she said, "Again I ask you to please repeat the words after me: 'Dear Jesus, if I take another drink, I will become sick unto death.'"

With a voice shaking with deep-felt emotion, he said those words that would change his life forever! When he finished, the congregation applauded as his mother-in-law hugged him and wept.

The Rest of the Story

One year later, this man told me, "Jimmie, the rest of the story is that from that moment on I have not had another drink. My wife and children are back with me, and these roses are for Miss Kuhlman because Jesus used her for my deliverance."

I later discovered that each man on that stage brought roses to the service on the anniversary of his deliverance.

Every time these men sang, the whole audience would stand to their feet, weeping and cheering, because these men were truly singing songs from their hearts.

Kathryn's Productions

Kathryn Kuhlman had the rare ability of making the gospel easily understandable by "staging" it. She would use lighting effects in such a dynamic way that it would cause you to see the gospel message in a whole new way. She was often criticized for this, but I believe that God had given her both the talent and vision for how this should be done.

I have witnessed different types of evangelism, but I grew to appreciate Kathryn's style. For example, her Christmas productions were marvelous events. Each year, she ordered and had delivered to the auditorium 50 Christmas trees, each 60 feet tall, and then had them decorated with 3,000 to 4,000 lights. The night of the program, the choir was clad in "biblical dress," and the men of the choir all had real beards, which they had spent weeks growing before the production, so that they would have the touch of authenticity.

Doing a Christmas program with Kathryn was not always without its problems however. I happened to be present one year when she decided to use live animals. There were sheep, cows, goats, birds, and a donkey. It was quite a menagerie and proved to be a bit difficult to manage.

Kathryn had insisted that the donkey be there for "Mary" to ride upon. The donkey, however, was a temperamental "actor," and when the time came for the first performance, apparently he was unhappy with his role or else was just having a bad day, and he "missed his cue."

The problem started when the stage hands, who had just gotten the donkey halfway up the steps at the side of the stage, stopped to take a breather. When they tried to move him again, the donkey dug in his heels and refused to budge. The men got behind it and pushed, while others pulled from the front, but the donkey had decided that it was not moving and began to kick and make "donkey sounds."

Kathryn was the narrator for this particular Christmas event, and she stood at the side of the stage, delivering what we call today "an illustrated sermon" or, as it was described at my Bible school, "preaching the parables." She read the solemn cue for the entrance of Mary, but no donkey arrived on stage. Kathryn was not deterred, and she recited the line several times over.

When the donkey still did not appear, someone slipped Kathryn a note that said the donkey was refusing to go up onto the stage. After reading this, Kathryn's face lit up like a lamp. "Well," she told the audience, "I have been told that the donkey won't come up the stairs. I guess I should have laid hands on it and rebuked that 'spirit of stubbornness' before we started."

The place erupted into uncontrollable laughter, and Kathryn later used this story in her sermons on stubbornness; but that was the first and last year that she used live animals.

The Communion Service

Kathryn also used creative lighting very effectively for communion services. She only held a communion service twice a year at her church—at Easter and on New Year's Day.

As the service began, the platform curtain would open to reveal men (who were choir members and ushers) standing shoulder to shoulder, three or four deep. Each of them wore a black tie and suit and had a flower in his lapel.

In front of them were several long, banquet-style tables that went from one end of the platform to the other. On these tables, the silver communion trays were stacked, and in between each stack of trays were candelabras, each holding seven white candles. As the stage lights were lowered, the flames that flickered from the candles seemed to lend a powerful aura of solemnity to the occasion.

Kathryn stood in the middle of all this, wearing a white chiffon dress, and as she began to speak, the spotlight "spotted" her in silhouette. Starting in a low, spiritual tone and gradually speeding up, she repeated the immortal words of Isaiah: "He was wounded for our transgressions, bruised for our iniquities...."

The choir began to sing softly, "Oh, the Blood of Jesus," and then I took the microphone and sang "At the Cross."

After I finished, the stage lights came back on and Kathryn was in full view. While the choir again sang, she ceremoniously lifted each stack of trays, which contained the "bread and wine," from the table and deposited them into the hands of the men standing there, many of whom were still singing.

When she was finished handing out the trays, Kathryn nodded her head and clasped her hands in a prayerful manner, not wanting her personality to overshadow the sacredness of this wonderful moment. Then the men went into the audience to serve "the bread and the wine."

As the people were being served, Kathryn said, "His body was broken and bruised for us," and then gave the command for them to not eat or drink until everyone had been served.

After everyone was served, Kathryn said, "Would you take the bread and break it together."

As I broke my piece of crusty bread, and heard the sound of bread cracking in the hands of 3,000 people simultaneously, I could almost imagine hearing the sound of Jesus' bones breaking on the cross at Calvary.

Then Kathryn said, "Please drink the wine together."

She had once again demonstrated a talent for using production, whether it was music or the spoken word, to bring glory to the Lord.

Chapter Four

"Elmer Gantry" or for Real?

*O*N THE EARLY DAYS of my association with Kathryn Kuhlman, there were times when I harbored serious doubts about how legitimate she actually was. I would stand on the stage a few feet from her and observe her famous histrionics, her over-the-top enunciation, her dramatic gestures, and the fantastic healings and want to shake my head with what I was seeing.

The film *Elmer Gantry,* which starred Burt Lancaster as a preacher and con man, had recently come out, and I began to wonder if Kathryn was, indeed, just a female version of this character.

I even began to wonder if she had planted actors and actresses in the audience who just pretended they had been healed and then would "take the money and run!"

You have to remember that during that period of my Christian life, I was still laboring under my conservative theological teaching—or should I say, mis-teaching.

So I decided to do my own private investigation of Miss Kuhlman. I began by talking to some of the people who were loyal to her, people who worked in jobs that never allowed them to be in the spotlight or even to receive a good salary. These people appeared to be content to work behind the scenes, in the shadows.

Shooting From the Hip

Charles C. Loesch, who had been Kathryn Kuhlman's chauffeur, maintenance man, and factotum for many years, was such a person. He was a man's man, the kind of person you could not just push around, yet he would do anything that Kathryn asked him to do, however menial it appeared.

One day I found "Loesch," as we all called him, pacing around outside Kathryn's dressing room at CBS. He spent hours there protecting the door from unwanted visitors.

This day, however, he was not his usual congenial self. He was mumbling something under his breath and appeared to be very upset.

"What's wrong?" I asked him.

Loesch stopped, looked at me, then hissed, "These cynics make me sick." His voice then rose several decibels.

"They are always finding something wrong with Miss Kuhlman and the ministry," he almost shouted with passion. "They don't know that lady. They don't know what she did for me!"

"Really!" I said with feigned surprise. Loesch had peaked my interest, since I was dying to find out if the healings were actually fakes.

"Yes," he continued, breathing heavily and by now crimson-faced. "I was a wreck when she came into my life. I was all bent over."

As long as I had known him, he had stood tall and straight as a ramrod, and I watched with my jaw agape.

"Oh yes, I was bent over and used to have to walk like this," he said as he began to "make like" the Hunchback of Notre Dame.

As he did this, my eyes suddenly filled with tears because, for a moment, I forgot about how straight he now stood. While he told me the rest of his story, he continued to walk around, bent over in a grotesque manner.

"I walked like this after being injured in an accident," said Charles, hardly able to mouth the words because of his deep-felt emotion. "My sacroiliac had become calcified, causing me to walk in a stooped position, bent forward from the hip in this manner, for 14 years. It was like my bones had been fused together," he explained.

He looked at me and got angry.

"You don't believe me," he railed gruffly, flapping his hands in frustration.

I caught him by the arm because I thought he was about to walk away.

When I convinced him of my interest in learning, he went on with inscrutable certainty, "One of my legs was three and three-quarter inches shorter than the other, so I had to wear a special shoe with a built-up sole. I was in constant pain since that accident."

Loesch said that his children had heard about Kathryn Kuhlman and had encouraged him to go to her miracle services, both in Pittsburgh and Franklin.

"At the first one, nothing happened. But on the way home, I stopped my car and poured all the liquor I had in the trunk out onto the highway and then threw away my cigars.

"I came to the second service feeling somehow different, cleaner. As I heard Miss Kuhlman preach, I forgot about my own problems and I focused my prayers on the people who were in worse shape than me."

He paused for a moment, so I jumped in and asked, "Then what happened?"

He was irritated by my interjection.

"Don't interrupt me," he said impatiently. Charles Loesch was the kind of person that you did not rush for anything. He was very meticulous in what he did and how he articulated himself.

When he saw the apologetic look on my face, he continued. "It happened one afternoon in Faith Temple when Miss Kuhlman was again preaching. My leg began to vibrate, hitting the floor like an air hammer."

"Vibrate like an air hammer?" I repeated as I felt my throat become dry.

"Please don't interrupt me," he snapped again.

"But I want to hear the next of the story, for I had no idea what the Lord had done for you."

His brow again furrowed with irritation.

"If you'll just keep quiet and let me talk for a little while, I'll tell you the story," he said acidly.

With a watery smile, I promised to hold my tongue.

Satisfied with my response, he continued his narrative: "Kathryn stopped her sermon and asked, 'What was that noise?'"

Remembering that moment, he added, "Man, I was never so embarrassed in all my life, so I bent over and held on to my leg to try and stop it from hitting the floor.

"Then Miss Kuhlman looked across at me and said, 'You are healed, sir!' She then turned to the audience and said, 'The power of God is on this man.'"

Loesch then revealed to me that he had stood up, and his back was straight, loose, and limber.

"I've been working for Miss Kuhlman for about 28 years now and nobody will ever make me believe anything bad about this wonderful woman," he said, his eyes shining with pride.

I was astonished with what I had just heard. I heaved a sigh of relief. He had made me a believer in Kathryn Kuhlman. I had heard the truth directly from someone who had been miraculously healed under her ministry.

I watched Loesch closely from then on and, with stinging eyes, noticed that whenever Kathryn was praying for a man with an addiction, a gleam appeared in his eyes as he whispered a prayer for that person. It was as if he was a private cheering team "putting it to" that man.

It was Charles Loesch who helped me stop to ask the questions about Kathryn Kuhlman. From then on, I was a true believer.

The Great Collector

Kathryn was a great collector of things. She amassed valuable antiques, beautiful art pieces, and quality jewelry. I believe that these magnificent *objets d'art*, which were worth hundreds of thousands of dollars, were her attempt to fill the void of not having a normal life and being such a high profile person.

Many of these items were given to her by supporters, and they included rare antiques and paintings from Europe, sculptures from Italy and South America, rugs from Iran (Persia) and the Far East, and diamonds and other precious jewels from around the world.

After gathering these priceless objects, she often gave them away. Although many people misunderstood this gesture, those who really knew Kathryn realized that when she gave a gift, she was not trying to buy the affection of that person, but rather she was giving away a part of herself that was precious and meaningful. In essence, Kathryn was saying, "I want you to have this because I appreciate you and value your ministry to the Lord."

On several occasions, I had the opportunity to visit her home at Fox Chapel, located on the outskirts of Pittsburgh, and received a guided tour of her house. As she proudly showed me her paintings, jewelry, and antiques, Kathryn had the most tender look in her eyes, almost as if she were talking about a child or a loved one. When she picked up an antique item, she would explain the history of it and then replace it on a shelf. She would then stand back and look at it for a moment. Oftentimes she reached over and straightened it about half an inch. It was as if she, the mother, were "dressing" a lapel or button of her child.

But though Kathryn was very fond of these collected items, there was one thing that she valued above all else—the dog-eared, stained Bible that she held aloft when she preached. Maybe that says everything about the ministry of Kathryn Kuhlman; for, more than anything, it was based on God's sacred Word.

Perpetual Motion

Kathryn Kuhlman lived her life in perpetual motion. Even her prayer life was carried out in a frenetic mode.

I often observed her pacing the floor in the area behind stage before her "miracle services." She was quite a sight as she walked up and down the floor, praying out loud, her arms flailing, "Dear Jesus, we just give You thanks. We praise You for Your anointing and...."

Then Kathryn would suddenly spot one of her staff members and, stopping her prayer in midstream, would tell them, "Please go and check that the air-conditioning is working properly in the auditorium."

As that person rushed off to obey her order, Kathryn would continue with her time of prayer. "Dear Jesus, I give you all the praise and glory."

A few minutes later, Kathryn would see another person on her staff and give the same instruction. For some reason, she always seemed to be concerned that the temperature in the hall was "just right."

Then her prayer time would resume. In other words, she was in a constant state of praying, but even then, she would stop time and again to ask questions about the arrangements for the upcoming meeting. Often Kathryn would send three or four people to get answers to the same question. I never figured out if this was a nervous reaction on her part, or if she was so caught up in what she was doing that she forgot she had already sent someone else.

When asked, on one occasion, how many hours a day she spent in prayer, I heard Kathryn reply, "I pray all the time, because if I limited the Holy Spirit to a certain number of hours a day, I would be in danger of using Him for my own purpose."

Kathryn paused briefly and added, "If, for instance, I spent one hour a day in prayer, I would expect the Holy Spirit to reward me for that hour. I would begin to feel that it was that hour in prayer that caused the 'anointing' in the meeting.

"No, I cannot use the Holy Spirit in that way. I must practice His presence all of the time."

It was not uncommon for Kathryn to walk and pray and hold intermittent conversations all within a few minutes.

When I first saw her praying in this way, I didn't want to interrupt her. However, this was taken out of my hands one day when she spotted me and walked over and began chatting. I stood rooted to the spot, not quite sure how I should react.

I discovered that our discourse was over when she suddenly walked away and began pacing the floor again and saying loudly, "Dear Jesus, I thank you...."

It was at times like these that I came to recognize that Kathryn's life was one of 24-hour-a-day relationship with Jesus. She had no success formulas, no methods or techniques; she just walked, talked, and lived as a powerful woman in the service of her God.

As a matter of fact, when a service was over and hundreds of people had been miraculously healed during it, Kathryn had a way of making you feel that you were an important part of what had happened—that the Holy Spirit had used you as an extension of what He was doing. You felt that because of her encouraging words you were learning to trust Him more and more.

Kathryn Recognizes the Anointing in My Life

Additionally, Kathryn Kuhlman showed me that she recognized the "anointing" in my own life. Although many people were in awe of her, I always found that she was the kind of person that you could talk to if you felt that a problem had arisen between you.

I remember there was an occasion that I had become quite burdened, even to the point of wanting to leave the ministry, over what I felt was a crucial matter. This problem was eating me up. I was becoming physically and emotionally drained, and I wrestled with how to bring up this situation with her. I began to pray that an opening would come, and shortly after, my prayer was answered.

Kathryn walked by me and was in her usual mode of pacing and praying out loud. Even though she had just given me a quick glance, she obviously sensed that there was a problem.

She stopped me and asked pointedly, "What's wrong, Jimmie?"

The feeling of disquiet inside of me intensified. I didn't know if this was the right time or not to launch into my dissertation. For a long moment, the tension inside me screwed itself up another notch. The silence spun out agonizingly. Then, I finally summoned up the courage to reveal what was on my mind.

The Wind-Up Toy

I took a deep breath and said, "Kathryn, if you really want to know, I have begun to feel like a wind-up toy. You always choose the music that you want me to sing. I realize that it is the kind of music that you are familiar with, but I want you to know that I always pray about the music and what I should sing, but you always tell me what I should sing."

"Yea!" was her bewildered response.

As she stood eyeball-to-eyeball with me, I told her, "The Spirit of God has sometimes troubled me all night to such an extent that I could not sleep, baptizing me with the phrases and sentences and stanzas that He wants me to sing."

I stopped, and I saw her look of wide-eyed interest.

"I would then come to the auditorium and you would say, 'Here is what I want you sing.' It seems that you do not take into consideration that I must spend time before the Lord to receive an anointing for my participation.

"As a result of your decisions, I have been trying to please you but I have not been able to do my best."

Feeling anxious and self-conscious, I pointed out that the evidence of this was that I had sometimes forgotten the words of the song "because my heart has not been in it."

I then told Kathryn, "Someone asked a well-known voice teacher about the performance of a famous female singer, 'What do you think of the tenor of her voice?' He replied, 'She has a wonderful voice and sings well but if I had anything to do with her, I would give her a broken heart.' "

Kathryn looked at me as if she didn't understand the point I was making.

"You cannot sing of pain and deliverance unless you have experienced pain and deliverance," I explained. "Only when you have that heart hunger, and have felt the disappointed hopes, the silent waiting, the holding of your peace when you want to speak, can you put your all into a song.

"This is the way the Holy Spirit teaches you to sing your phrases."

Her eyes now locked onto mine and she was beginning to follow my line of reasoning.

"My own voice teacher always told me, 'Jimmie, sing with a head like a keg of ice and a heart like a raging furnace.' "

Her eyes lit up.

"What you are saying, Jimmie, is that you don't just sing songs, you have to feel them from your very being."

"That's right, Kathryn. And that's what I want to do from now on."

"Oh, Jimmie," she exclaimed in a soft, placatory tone, "I never knew you felt like that. Thank you for sharing this with me."

With tears in her eyes, she hugged me. Then, with a voice that cracked with deep-felt emotion, Kathryn whispered, "Jimmie, I would never want to do anything to quench the Spirit in my life or yours." A look of infinite sadness had spread across Kathryn's face.

As she released her embrace, she patted me on the shoulders and I heaved a great sigh of relief.

She said, "I have to explain that the only reason I have told you what to sing was because for many years I've had singers who never flowed with me in the ministry. I was just a 'tool' in their hands."

Kathryn Kuhlman proved to me by her reaction to my comments what a big person she was. She agreed to consult me in the future about the kind of music that I would sing at her meetings. From then on, she would say to me; "Mr. Jimmie, what have you been praying about today?" I would then share with her the song that had come to mind and she usually agreed with it for me to sing that night.

Free From Bondage

Kathryn Kuhlman's attitude had loosed me from the bondage I had been feeling, but it also gave me a new sense of responsibility. I now was singing with the newfound freedom that I felt in the Holy Spirit.

The liberation was exhilarating for me. There were times that, when the song was over, I would sit down totally overcome with emotion. My heart would be pounding so fast that I sometimes thought I was having a heart attack.

The Lord began to show me that if you have not "experienced a song" in your mind, your heart, and your spirit, you cannot communicate its message to someone else, no matter how popular it may have been on the hit music charts.

Woken Up by the Holy Spirit

There were times after this when the Holy Spirit would awaken me at two or three o'clock in the morning, and a song would begin to move about in my head, and I would sing it out loud. That same song would often come to me in my dressing room at the CBS studios. I would lay on a couch and feel the lyrics literally go through my body. The Holy Spirit would burn them into my mind, and I would understand what the "song poet" had in mind when he or she wrote the song.

When the knock would come on my door for me to come on to the stage, I would feel the anointing so strong that I was concerned I might "go down" before the power before I even got out onto the set.

I would say to myself, "Please, Mr. Director, mark my spot so that I can get this song out of me before I burst or just melt and become a black wet spot."

I came to believe that the same anointing was on me in the ministry of music that was on Kathryn Kuhlman when she began speaking.

Not only did this "special anointing" come at the TV studios, but it also came at the Shrine meetings.

However, there were times that I did come up dry about what I should sing, and it was at those times that Kathryn would say, "Jimmie, I have something that I'd like you to do."

The relationship was one of mutual respect for the anointing on each of our lives.

Chapter Five

A Sea of Pain

FTER I HAD ACCEPTED that Kathryn Kuhlman's ministry was indeed for real, I began a ritual that would prepare me for the upcoming service. I would go to the dressing room, take a shower, put on my stage clothes, and then wander around the auditorium as the crowds poured in. As I did, I would ask the Holy Spirit to "impact" my own mind and spirit about what lay ahead during another "Evening of Miracles."

My heart would literally break as I would see the hordes of people in wheelchairs being pushed in by loving relatives, while others were being stretchered in, and even more were limping into that arena with every kind of illness imaginable.

It was a vast "Sea of Pain," but I was comforted by my now firm belief that, for many, a healing was going to take place, maybe not immediately, but I was confident that it would occur.

I never realized, however, that on one evening, in a major Texas town, my heart would be broken over a situation that confronted me, and my belief would be truly tested.

A Test of Faith

As I walked through the auditorium on that fateful night, I noticed that every seat had already been taken. The local fire marshals were there, carrying clipboards and checking to see if any of the fire codes were being violated in this huge hall.

I smiled when I noticed people putting coats and Bibles on their seats as they went to the concession stands to get hot dogs or pay a visit to the rest room. They did this so that nobody would steal their seats.

I then walked out to the entrance area where the glass doors had already been locked tight, and saw hundreds of desperate faces pressed up against the glass. Their eyes all seemed to be saying, "Please let us into the auditorium," but I knew it was too late. The place was already filled to capacity.

Then I heard thunderous applause coming from inside the arena, and I rushed to see workers assisting a woman out of a wheelchair who was shouting, "I've been healed." People were on their feet, shouting and praising God for the miracle that had already taken place before the service had even begun.

The choir began practicing their songs of praise to the Lord, and even during the rehearsal period the atmosphere was so electric that I could hardly bear it.

"Thank you, Jesus," was all I could say as I rejoiced with them.

Through the Glass

I turned again and walked out to where the people were still crushed against the glass doors. It was then that I spotted a woman lying on a stretcher, an IV drip in her arm and an oxygen bottle with a tube that ran to her nose helping her breathe. Her face was paper-white except for the dark circles under her eyes. She looked about as sick as a person can get.

The man who was with her began urgently rapping on the window and mouthed to me, "May I speak to you for one moment?"

I pushed my way through the throng of people and was stopped several times by those who recognized me. I tried to be polite to them, but I kept pressing on. When I got to the door, I asked the security officer to "open it" for me. He did so just a crack and I leaned through.

With tears in his eyes, the man explained, "I've come from California with my sister and my wife, who is lying on the stretcher. We hired an ambulance to bring us from the airport because my wife has been told that she has only one month to live, and we are desperate for her to get into the service." Her disease was so powerful that this was the only thing he could offer his wife.

The man wiped away the tears with his coat sleeve and then said, "We've been here for three hours, but the auditorium filled up before we were able to get in. I'm begging you, sir. Please help us. Is there any way you can get us inside?"

Then he added, "The Lord told me to ask you."

I was speechless. I knew there had been times when people would tack on "The Lord has told me" to what they were asking. I considered this a kind of spiritual blackmail. However, I felt on this occasion that the man was telling the truth.

I summoned an usher who was hovering nearby and said, "Would you please assist these three people inside and then follow me."

He nodded and told a security man to open the door. As they moved forward, I noticed that some of the black people outside were glaring at me, as if to say, "My color is your color, and yet you are passing us up for these people who happen to be white." I understood their frustration, but at that moment, I felt that I had to do something to help these people.

But then came another problem. As they were trying to come through the door, another usher intervened and said to me in a brusque manner, "I'm sorry, sir, but they can't come in."

Pulling Rank

My friends looked confused and concerned. Then I did something I would not normally do. I "pulled rank" on this man.

Taking his arm, I told the burly usher, "I'm Jimmie McDonald and I'm with Miss Kuhlman."

He stared at me in mute surprise, and his attitude changed immediately. "Please forgive me," he said. "I did not recognize you."

Then he added, "You can see that the place is completely full. Where shall I put them?"

The husband then came into the conversation. "My sister and I will stay out here," he said through the slit in the doorway, "if only you will get my wife inside the building."

I rubbed my chin and then replied, "No, we'll try and get all of you in, even if it means that you have to sit on the platform."

As I stood there, I sent up an ejaculatory prayer to Heaven: "Help!"

With that, the door was opened and the couple carried the woman inside on her stretcher. We found a locale by a wall, and they gently lowered her to the floor and stood by her.

Then I left them and went onto the stage to join Kathryn who was already in "full swing." After a short time, I sang, and I looked in the direction of this California threesome, trying to show them that this worship song was for them.

Puppy-Dog Eyes

The service came to an end and many people had been healed, but not the woman on the stretcher. As I left the stage, I wandered amongst the people and shook hands with many there, hoping against hope that they would leave and I would not have to face those six, sad, puppy-dog eyes, knowing that I had nothing to say to them.

But, as the crowd began to thin out, I felt the Spirit of the Lord saying to me, "Go back and speak to them."

I tried to push this out of my mind because I didn't think I should pray for her healing just then. That may seem strange, but I felt this way because Kathryn often said during a service, "Some of you were healed before the meeting, others during it, and some will be healed on the way home."

She used to say this because some people would attempt to utilize the Kathryn Kuhlman meetings to establish their own gifts or even to exploit them. I never wanted to be accused of these things. I also believed that you could become a hindrance to the working of the Holy Spirit because He has the perfect timing and place for each miracle to take place. It was not something that we could control.

Because of this conviction, I was a little leery about going back to the group. However, when I approached them, the husband took me by the hand and thanked me warmly. But when I looked at the woman lying on the stretcher, my heart dropped, as I could see the hope draining from her face.

I took the man by the hand and said, "Sir, I'm going to ask you a very unusual request. Could you come back tomorrow night?"

His face was full of anguish. He closed his eyes and shook his head tiredly. "I don't think so," he replied weakly.

I was surprised with his response. "But, why not?" I asked.

"We've come all this way and its been rough on my wife," he said in a voice that was high and despairing. "I don't think we could bear any more disappointment; and on top of that, I don't think we could find a hotel for us to stay in. Everywhere seems to be full."

I thought for a moment and then said, "I believe God has a hotel room for you. Why don't you get your sister to go and make a few calls on the payphone and see if she can find a room."

As we anxiously awaited her return, I told the couple, "I really believe you need to come back tomorrow night."

The man still wasn't convinced, however. "I thank you for your beautiful concern, Mr. McDonald," he said, "but I don't want to put my wife through this ordeal again. We could stand in line again and then find that we can't get in."

I tried to counter his concern by saying, "Sir, if you come back, I will make sure that when the doors are opened you will be the first ones to get in."

Even as I uttered these words, the lady returned with a smile on her face. "We've got a room!" she exclaimed.

With that, I shook their hands and I looked at the gaunt, dying woman, who looked as if she knew it was now the end of her life. I laid my hands on her forehead on the stretcher, not in prayer, but as an affirmation that I was believing with her for her miracle to take place.

The following evening, I was busy in my dressing room preparing for the program ahead and, I have to confess, had completely forgotten about my promise.

My thoughts were disturbed when a knock came on the door.

"Come in," I called out loudly.

An usher peeked through and told me, "Brother McDonald, there are some people at the front door who said that you would get them in. What should I do?"

I followed him out, and we went to the door where he pointed out my three friends, who were again part of a huge crowd people who couldn't get in.

The husband waved desperately at me, and I told the usher, "Yes, by all means, let them in."

The Prayer of Faith

As they gratefully pushed through the people, carrying the woman on the stretcher, I mouthed a prayer: "Lord, I thank You for bringing them back tonight, and I praise You for the healing You are going to bring to this woman tonight."

But still, as I looked at the woman, the prognosis did not look good. She was even paler than she had been the day before. Her eyes had visibly sunk into their sockets and were surrounded by circles so dark that they looked like she had black eyes.

After making sure they were properly situated, I went onto the stage. As the service began, I just knew that this woman would be the first one to get off her stretcher.

So, throughout the service, each time Kathryn Kuhlman told people to "just receive your healing," I kept my eyes fixed on the woman. Kathryn would continue by saying, "Get up out of your wheelchair or stretcher. Move your legs; move your necks."

People across the auditorium began to be healed, but still this lady lay motionless on her stretcher as if she were dead. Even from my vantage point, I could see that her face had an alarmingly bluish cast with deep maroon-colored lips.

I knew how Kathryn's meetings ended. She would invite people who wanted to "get saved" to move forward to the front of the platform. As she issued this invitation, people began to run to the front and soon were praying the "sinner's prayer" with her.

I looked back and saw the woman was still on her stretcher, and my heart began to break for her and her family.

Kathryn then thanked the chairman of the crusade, the person who had arranged for the music, the ushers, and she even asked people to write to their local newspaper to thank them for the "wonderful way" they had "covered" the crusade.

Then she asked everyone to bow their heads for the benediction. After the prayer was completed and Kathryn had said "Amen," I took one final look at the woman on her stretcher; she still lay there prone and desperate. She hadn't been healed!

As I walked off the stage, tears began to sting my eyes. "Lord," I prayed, "what happened?"

I was suddenly halted as I heard people begin to shout out, "Hallelujah! Praise the Lord!"

I ran back on stage and looked through the curtain that was now closed and saw the woman getting off the stretcher. She was taking the oxygen apparatus off her face and the IV drip from her arm. She shuffled, then walked, toward the stage to the thunderous applause of those who were witnessing this great miracle. The bedridden patient was healed!

The choir began to sing the "Battle Hymn of the Republic." Those words, "Glory, glory, hallelujah, His truth is marching on," were to me so true for that incredible moment.

I walked away from that experience knowing that if God could and would heal, it would be in His own timing.

Chapter Six

I Believe in Miracles

I BLINKED WITH DISBELIEF as I saw the slight figure of Bette Davis walk slowly into that CBS television studio in Hollywood and take a seat in the shadows with other members of the audience. This American movie legend, who had twice won an Academy award, for *Dangerous* (1935) and *Jezebel* (1938), was taking some time out from making a film in a nearby studio to watch Kathryn tape another episode of her *I Believe in Miracles* show that had taken America by storm.

As I stood by the side of the set, I found it hard to take my eyes off Miss Davis, and I noticed that as Kathryn spoke about Jesus and His plan of salvation, she dabbed her eyes with her handkerchief.

During a brief stop in the taping, I summoned up the courage to slip over to the seat next to her and shake her hand.

"I'm Jimmie McDonald, Miss Kuhlman's singer," I told her. Bette Davis smiled and turned to face me.

"I'm so glad to meet you, Mr. McDonald," she said in her deep, inimitable voice.

Although this woman was one of the most well-known actresses of all time, I realized that, like all of us, she too had spiritual needs and was obviously seeking the answer to life's most pressing question: how to have one's sins forgiven!

Bette Davis Eyes

"Miss Davis, would you like to meet Miss Kuhlman?" I whispered.

Her porcelain-like face lit up and her famous "Bette Davis eyes" shone.

"Oh yes!" she replied, "but I don't want to distract her right now."

I assured Miss Davis that when the next break came, I would go over to Kathryn and ask if she could come and meet her. A few minutes later, the opportunity presented itself when Kathryn stopped for a change in the lighting position. I got up from my seat and went over to her.

"Yes, Jimmie," she said.

"Miss Kuhlman, Bette Davis is sitting in the audience and would love to meet you."

Kathryn's face came alive. "Oooh, I'd loove to meeeet her," she enthused in her Missouri cornbread accent.

So I went back to Bette Davis and escorted her over to where Kathryn was seated.

"Hi there, hooooney," gushed Kathryn as Miss Davis sat down next to her. "I am soo honored that you would come to my taping."

Bette Davis told her that she had watched her for years. "Your show is such a blessing to me," said the actress. "I had a few minutes to spare and so I thought I would come and see you in person."

Kathryn beamed with pride and then asked, "Would you like me to pray with you, deeear?"

Miss Davis nodded her head, and with that, Kathryn Kuhlman clasped Bette Davis's hand and prayed for "God's blessing" on her life. Miss Davis again dabbed her eyes and thanked her for the prayer.

Bette Davis had once starred in a movie called *The Lonely Life,* and I wondered if she was, indeed, a lonely person. Many people did not realize how difficult it was for stars like her to have a private life. They thought that everything was wonderful for them. But in fact, most stars knew they were only playing roles that a scriptwriter had penned for them, while their own lives were often empty. Kathryn, however, knew that the only real role that people could play was already scripted for them in the Bible.

There were many other stars who came into the studio and watched the tapings. These included Robert Young and Carol Channing. I believe that the Hollywood stars were attracted to Kathryn because she had been catapulted into a "star position" through her hit television program. At the CBS studios, she brought in as many people to be her "live" audience as the big stars did for their shows. So these celebrities looked at her as a fellow star.

I am not sure how many of these people truly understood her message though. Unfortunately, some probably just saw her as someone who had become a major figure in American life, so they gave her the respect they thought was her due.

Dinah Shore

One of the wonderful advantages we had from working on a major television show is that it afforded us the opportunity to visit some of the other shows that were being taped there. Since the same crew that was taping Kathryn's show interchanged with the others, such as *The Dinah Shore Show,* they already knew many of the personalities we had on *I Believe in Miracles.*

One day, having a few minutes to spare before I did my song for Kathryn's program, I decided to wander into one of the other sets. I stopped when I saw the sign, "The Dinah Shore Show," on one of the doors.

Since the red light was not on, I stepped inside, and I saw one of the crew members who was also working on Kathryn's show.

"Hi, Jimmie," he smiled. "Do you like the set?"

I nodded.

"Hey, do you want to meet Dinah?"

As I smiled, he grabbed me by the hand and took me over to meet her.

"Dinah," he said as we stood in front of her, "this is Jimmie McDonald who works with Kathryn Kuhlman."

Her face lit up. "I'm very pleased to meet you, Mr. McDonald," she said, shaking my hand. "Please tell Kathryn that we love her and that we are proud of the fact that she is a part of the CBS family."

I promised to tell her this.

Yes, Kathryn Kuhlman was treated like a star, but she never acted like one.

A Down-to-Earth Star

Naturally, Kathryn understood that *I Believe in Miracles* was not just her own ministry show; it had to reflect the CBS standard. So when they insisted that one of their clothing designers take charge of creating her gowns, Kathryn agreed.

This lady designer would often bring her latest "creations" to Kathryn to see which ones she liked. Many times I was there with Kathryn, discussing some aspect of the taping, and would watch the way she would painstakingly look at each one of the creations and say something positive about each of them. This was her way of protecting the designer from any potential fear that she might have.

Kathryn would then take the garments into her dressing room—which, incidentally, had a star on the door—and put them on, one at a time. Then, she would come out to me and ask, "What do you think, Jimmie?"

Often Kathryn thought the gowns were too glamorous, and she would turn them down, saying, "You know I can't wear this. I'm a preacher!"

Sometimes we had to coax Kathryn into wearing some of the ensembles. One of us would say to her, "Remember, Kathryn, that God has placed a 'preacher' in a beautiful female body."

Kathryn would then blush and usually agree to wear the outfit.

At the end of the day, we would all gather with Dick Ross, her producer, who had produced many of

Billy Graham's films, in one of the screening rooms and view all the shows that were done that day. (We would usually do a month's worth of programs over a two-day period.) Kathryn was a perfectionist, and she would sometimes be loudly critical of her own "performance." But on other occasions, she would sit and weep over what she had seen in what she believed to be the wonderful presence of the Holy Spirit.

At the end of the tapings of 100 shows, the local custom was that the star put on a celebration with cakes and drinks, usually champagne. However, because Kathryn was a teetotaler and wanted to be a witness for Christ around the crew, she told them that she would only supply Koolaid and Ginger Ale. But they didn't seem to mind.

Kathryn Kuhlman was definitely treated like a star. As a matter of fact, CBS had a "director's chair" inscribed with her name on it and had placed it in the studio, but she found this to be embarrassing.

"Jimmie, why don't you sit in my chair until it's time for you to come on the set," she would often tell me.

Kathryn made sure that every person on the staff was taken care of, and she would listen to us when we had a difficulty. For instance, in those days, a good makeup that matched all the different skin tones for black people had not yet been perfected. Consequently, I had difficulty finding makeup that suited me.

"Kathryn," I told her one day, "I have discovered a place in New York that can provide the kind of makeup that I need."

She smiled and said, "Get it, Jimmie, and send me the bill!"

Kathryn would not rest until I had the makeup that I was comfortable with. "We must have the best for Jesus" was her explanation.

Still, she was "the boss." Kathryn would listen to the advice of the program directors, and then make up her own mind as to what she should do regarding her show.

Kathryn's effusive personality made her popular with the stage crew. These were thorough professionals who were used to working for big-name personalities and knew all about temper tantrums. But they didn't see these from Kathryn and appeared to be completely at ease and relaxed around her.

Sometimes, crew members would come up to Kathryn and put their arms around her shoulders during a break in the action. If she felt that their embrace was going to get out-of-line, she would gently, and with grace, move and adjust their embrace so that it had the level of warmth and meaning that she believed the person had intended it to have.

One day I reminded her that I had seen how she got out of that uncomfortable position and how proud of her I was. She threw back her head and laughed.

"Oh, Jimmie, you just see too much," she chuckled. "But you are right. We must honor Jesus at all times."

CBS Will Never Be the Same

Because of the way she carried herself in the studio, it was not unusual to see those men, who did not profess any church experience, weeping during her taping.

I even witnessed some of the crew members come up to her during a break and ask her to pray with them over a personal problem or ask if she would counsel one of their relatives who was in trouble. And there were times when the crew would bring their wives or children to have her pray over them for a healing.

I never saw Kathryn refuse to do any of these things. I would smile after she prayed for someone because she always commented, while swinging her arms together like a little girl, "Well, CBS will never be the same after that."

I would often see these same men at the Shrine Auditorium or hear them say, "We'll be there Sunday, Kathryn."

Kathryn was a real trouper and would try almost anything. I remember one day, one of the floor directors wanted to play a joke on Carol Burnett, so he asked Kathryn if she would help him. When she heard of the plot, Kathryn got that little girlish look in her eyes and said, "Yea. Why not!"

The man explained that Carol Burnett was always boasting to her co-stars that she always knew what was going on during her show and so she held the record of not being able to be "broken up" by anybody.

The floor director said, "Carol is supposed to say her line and open the door, and one of her co-stars is supposed to come out from behind the door. Instead, we would like you to come out and surprise her. We'll see then if we can finally break her up."

Kathryn thought this was extremely funny and agreed to do it. She crept into a next-door studio and stood waiting out of sight. On cue, Kathryn rapped at the "set" door, and when Carol Burnett called for the person to come out, Kathryn came through the door and onto the stage and said, "Have you been waiting for me?"

Carol Burnett finally "lost it" and fell to the floor laughing uncontrollably. This was, no doubt, partly because she would often "bring the house down" during her show with completely over-the-top Kathryn Kuhlman imitations.

I don't know whether or not this show ever got aired, but it became the talk of CBS studios, and showed just how human and down-to-earth Kathryn was.

The "Other" Kathryn Kuhlmans

Because of Kathryn's unique raspy voice and her dramatic hand gestures on television, she helped spawn an industry of impersonators. These comics were guaranteed huge laughs by impersonating her voice and the way she got up on her tiptoes and with diminutive, fleet steps, flitted backwards on the stage while she waved a finger in the air and said, "The Hooooly Spiiiirit is here," or "I give you gloooory. I give you praise."

Jamie Buckingham once wrote:

"Her 1940s hair style...all lent themselves to the idea exaggerated caricature people loved to imitate. One Hollywood movie producer, a

Jewish person, was a great fan of Kathryn's. He said she had all the makings of a star since she was the only woman in the world who could turn the word 'God' into four syllables."[3]

Probably the most outlandish imitation of Kathryn came from Ruth Buzzi on the enormously successful *Laugh In* show when she would "lay hands" on casaba melons in a supermarket.

On one occasion, Kathryn saw this and thought it was the funniest thing she had ever seen. As a matter of fact, she sent a personal letter to Ruth Buzzi in which she said, "No one enjoyed the satire more than I."

Ms. Buzzi responded by sending Kathryn two dozen long-stemmed roses, but then stopped doing the impersonation, something we all regretted.

Chapter Seven

In the Presence of the Lord

KATHRYN KUHLMAN was a person who truly understood what the word worship meant, for she was keenly aware that through worship, you could enter the very presence of the Lord. From my 15 years with her, I can attest to the fact that Kathryn walked, talked, and breathed worship in all that she did.

Although Kathryn was best-known for her healing services, she was well aware that there was more to physical healing than just making a sick body well. To her there was the possibility of that person then growing into a deeper, personal relationship with God by handing that healed life over to Jesus Christ and experiencing the "new birth."

You see, Kathryn Kuhlman held that the main purpose of healing was to lead the person God had touched to not just live a life that was no longer painful, but also enter into the very presence of the third Person of the Trinity, the Holy Spirit—the One who facilitates the will of the Father and who is able to put feelings in action. These were the things that the

Father set in motion for us before the very foundation of the world.

A Hymn of Deliverance

The praise choruses that Kathryn used in her services were her way of expressing to the Lord the deep-felt feelings of love she had towards Him. As a mere mortal, she knew that through this music she, and all those participating with her, could have a heavenly experience.

I still remember the very first time I heard the singing of "How Great Thou Art" at a Kathryn Kuhlman crusade. Of course, I had heard it sung many times by the great Billy Graham crusade choirs and also by George Beverly Shea, but in Kathryn Kuhlman's meetings it seemed to take on a different meaning. I think this was because many of the people in her choir had been delivered by the Holy Spirit from terrible addictions, consequently, they were actually singing it as a personal love expression to the Lord for freeing them from their bondage.

For them, the only words that were adequate at that awesome moment were: *"Then sings my soul, my Savior God to Thee, how great Thou art."*

Free to Worship

One great writer, in penning his thoughts about such an experience, has said, "My long imprisoned soul has, at last, been set free to worship."

You knew, from the moment Kathryn Kuhlman moved onto the stage of a great auditorium like the Shrine, that she had come with one purpose in mind—to worship her Holy God.

Some of you might ask, "Why is worship necessary?" Well, my answer is that it is the mechanism that the Holy Spirit uses to lift us from the discontentment we may have experienced while waiting in one of those long lines to get into one of her services.

I was always surprised by the lengths that many people went to attend one of Kathryn Kuhlman's miracle services. Sometimes, people arrived early in the morning to make sure of their place in the building. As a matter of fact, on several occasions I drove by an auditorium and saw people who had been camped there all night just so they would be able to get in. These people were aware that the Holy Spirit would later take that momentary inconvenience and cause them to look past their physical condition, unto God Himself, because He had *all* that it was going to take to deal with the pain, or the ugliness of scars, and the inconvenience and cumbersomeness of a wheelchair.

The Great Escape

I believe that the Holy Spirit uses the worship time in a service to allow each one of us to momentarily escape those deep wounds of self-pity that so often make us feel uneasy.

Worship also allows one to say "no" to the negative words of the prognosticators of doom who have pronounced that "there is no hope!" The singing of these hymns and choruses shows that there *is* hope and that hope is found in Jesus Christ. It allows us to say, "Lord, it is nothing for you to make a new 'heart' inside of me, or to burn out the cancer in my body, or to lift me off of this stretcher, or to cause that ugly goiter on my throat to go down."

It is in a worship setting that miracles begin to take place. When we sing words like "I see the stars Your hands have made...You are an awesome God," we realize that if He could create the world, He could certainly deal with our greatest problems.

One of the songs I sang during Kathryn's services was "He Touched Me." I have to admit that I often had great difficulty completing this great worship song because I would be watching the hands of the "healing group workers" who were praying for sick people during this time, and then see the Holy Spirit "touching" the sickest of the sick at that very moment.

I witnessed people whose arms seemed to be rigidly stuck to their body begin to sing and, unconsciously, a movement or feeling would come into those arms and they would raise them in holy worship. The words of "He Touched Me" would often stick in my throat as I saw the surprised look on their faces.

Alleluia

One of the choruses we sang quite often was the "Alleluia" praise chorus. The first time I heard it was during one of the CBS tapings of Kathryn's *I Believe in Miracles* show. A group of young people, dressed like hippies, had come to the studio to meet Kathryn. They were quite a sight with their "love beads," psychedelic clothing, and long hair.

This incident occurred in the 1970's when the "Jesus People" movement was just beginning, and many of these young people had accepted Jesus as their Savior, but continued to dress in their freaky outfits. Chuck Smith of Calvary Chapel in Costa Mesa, California, had become the "father figure" of this movement, and singers like Larry Norman, with his long, flowing blond hair, were singing songs like "Why Should the Devil Have All the Good Music" and spending their spare time witnessing on Hollywood Boulevard.

One of the CBS security men went up to Kathryn during a break in the taping and told her that some 200 "hippies" had gathered in a nearby room and would like to meet with her. Being the gracious person that she was, Kathryn agreed.

Dino Kartsonakis, a wonderful pianist who had joined Kathryn's team, was also there in the studio. We were standing together and she said, "Jimmie and Dino, I want you to come with me."

As we walked into the room, the hippies began to sing praise choruses, and Kathryn just stood back and watched this wonderful event.

After they had finished their time of worship, Kathryn talked with them, and I could see that her motherly instinct was coming out. In her own inimitable way, she tilted her head to one side and that motherly, compassionate look came into her eye.

One of these "Jesus freaks," whose hair was even longer than the others', addressed Kathryn on behalf of the rest.

"Miss Kuhlman, we are all believers," he said. "God has rescued us from drugs, and we wondered if you would pray for us. We need a touch from God to help us continue in our walk with Him."

Tears welled up in Kathryn's eyes as she replied, "Of course, I will!"

With that, she began to pray for each of them, touching them on the forehead. As she did this, they began to sing "Alleluia," a chorus that we had never heard before. They sang it over and over again. It was one of the most blessed moments of my life.

These young people sang the chorus perfectly, even though they were not a professional or organized singing group. Some of them even began adding a descant. As they sang this descant melody, they sounded like a heavenly choir of angels heralding a special event.

As a professional musician, I had heard and sung the "Hallelujah Chorus" from Handel's *Messiah* many times. It had been uplifting and had affected me deeply. But this contemporary "Alleluia" praise and worship chorus had a different feeling. It was quiet and deeply personal worship without being cumbersome, and I found myself lifting up my hands.

As the singing continued, Kathryn moved amongst them and laid her hands on them. Many of them fell backwards to the floor as they were being "touched" by the power of the Holy Spirit.

Originally this was supposed to be just a time when these young people met with Kathryn Kuhlman, but it had proved so spiritually potent that Kathryn turned to Dick Ross, her TV producer, and said, "I know that we did not plan to do this, but could you add one more show, one with these young people? Please, let's do it, even if it means that we have to cancel something else."

She added, "I believe that we should show the power of God as He manifests Himself through these young people."

Dick agreed to the request, and he went into the studio to rearrange the set in order to get all of the young people on it.

I remember seeing the look on Kathryn's face as she stood in the middle of 200 "on fire" Christian hippies as they talked to her in front of the cameras about what the Lord had done for them.

Just before the taping was completed, Kathryn asked Dino if he would play the "Alleluia" praise chorus. Dino went over to the grand piano and began to play it, and once again we felt the power of the Lord as we all stood around the piano.

The chorus made such an impact on Kathryn that she had the choir in her church in Youngstown learn it. From that time on, it was sung in every crusade with the same result—the power of God's Spirit came down on the meeting.

Now, every time I hear it sung, my mind goes back to those long-haired, bearded boys, and those girls with their long dresses, which they wore to make a statement of their particular era. Little did these hippies know that they were introducing a chorus that would be sung around the world.

On one occasion while singing this little chorus, many people were healed. I heard an older lady sobbing over on the side, and when I turned to look at her, she was holding a neck brace in her hand, waving it and stating that she had been healed. I also saw people getting up out of wheelchairs.

I have learned that healing very often comes while we are worshiping the Lord. The unique thing about this particular chorus was that you did not have to learn the words. It could be sung in any language; it could be translated into any cultural tempo. I have heard it sung to the strumming of guitars or a cappella mode in a camp meeting. And in each instance God used it.

I don't know Jerry Sinclair, the man who wrote the chorus. All I know is that it has blessed people around the world. Alleluia. To God be the glory!

Chapter Eight

The Yielded Vessel

KATHRYN KUHLMAN was a driven woman, but that "drive" did not come from herself—it came from the Holy Spirit. She truly believed that she had become a "vessel of clay" for God's Spirit, someone who had been molded to do His will.

Kathryn, in one of her famous *Heart to Heart* radio talks, was "taking the lid off my [Kathryn's] heart" and baring things that few people know and "few will ever fully understand":

> "One of the greatest lessons that the whole world has to learn is how to yield oneself to the Holy Spirit. It's one of the hardest lessons that I have had to learn.

> "For I found out a long time ago that the Holy Spirit is not a person I can use, and that is the lesson. If only the Holy Spirit could get you to learn. He is not a person; He is not a power that I can use. He must use the vessel, for that is all that I can furnish.

"There is a place where one yields oneself completely to Him, where you give your body over to Him completely. Your body, your mind, your lips, your voice, and your consciousness are yielded completely over to Him, and all that He uses is the yielded vessel.

"I have never professed having any gift of the Spirit. I would not confess to you now that I have even one gift of the Spirit. There are those who have said that I have the gift of healing. There are those who have said that I have the gift of faith. You may have said it, but you'll never hear Kathryn Kuhlman profess to have any gift.

"I still contend that if one has been so honored of the Holy Spirit, if the Holy Spirit has so honored that one, has so entrusted that one with the gift, if He so willed to give one a gift or gifts of the Spirit, that one will treat that gift so carefully, will guard it so well, it will be such a treasured thing, that one will not talk about it or boast of it, for that one knows that it is a trust. It must be used carefully, wisely, discreetly; and along with the giving of that gift, there is a responsibility that is so great that it is almost overwhelming.

"Many a time have I stood on that top step, with a hand on that black doorknob, wishing that He'd called someone else instead of me.

"Many a time, I have been so overwhelmed with the knowledge that He has given me of the Word and the powers that are, with all that He has endowed me, and with the responsibility that He has entrusted me, that more than once I have envied that little woman on that Missouri farm who gathers the eggs at the close of the day from that little hen house, who perhaps helps with the milking, and who takes care of her precious little family. I could easily have been that farmer's wife in Missouri if God had not called me at the tender age of fourteen.

"She can go to bed at night tired, but she rests so well. And when the gray streaks of dawn break in the early morning hours, she again goes about her daily duties, a responsibility to her little family.

"But oh, the responsibility of one who has been called of God, the responsibility that goes with what He has entrusted one."

Kathryn, in this moving radio talk, expressed her feelings at the close of another miracle service:

"When I walk off the platform, I know those who leave that service must say, 'Miss Kuhlman must feel so well rewarded. Think of those who were healed of God in that great service.' And they go out of the hall almost with envy.

"But, beloved, I walk off that same platform thinking, 'Did I yield completely to the Spirit? If only I had known how to better cooperate with the Spirit, maybe another might have been healed. If only I had known how to better follow Him as He was moving in that great auditorium, someone else might have been set free."

Kathryn, with her voice cracking, explained that she was never out from under that great responsibility:

"The secret of those bodies that were healed in those miracle services is the power of the Holy Spirit, and the only part that I play is in yielding my body unto Him. He works through that body in lifting up Jesus, but the vessel must be yielded.

"I become completely detached from what happens during a miracle service. It is almost as if the person of Kathryn Kuhlman is seated with the crowd in the auditorium. As a person, I become completely separate from what the Holy Spirit is doing.

"Thousands have marveled that I can go through an entire service, sometimes as long as six hours, without stopping, always on my feet, never being seated once. And yet at the end, I can walk off that platform just as refreshed as I went on at the beginning of that service.

"Doctors have told me that from a medical standpoint it is impossible for any human body to take that beating, year in and year out. In fact, I can turn around and do it all again. I'll tell you the secret. It's because Kathryn Kuhlman doesn't do it. It's the power of the Holy Spirit.

"Let me preach an hour under the anointing of the Holy Spirit and I will walk off that stage more refreshed in body and mind than I was when I walked on that platform. There is refreshing for my own body as He fills the body with Himself and His own Spirit."

The Holy Spirit, Not Kathryn Kuhlman

I have actually witnessed this detachment that Kathryn Kuhlman was talking about. Standing there on the platform just a few feet away from her, I would see her eyes flash and dance with excitement as the Holy Spirit did His work through her.

She had a very interesting way of interviewing people who came onto the platform to share the healing they had just experienced.

Kathryn would ask, "What happened to you? What did you feel when you received your miracle? Is there now no pain?"

As the audience would cheer and clap, she would turn to the person and say, "Do everything you could not do before. Bend over. Do you feel any pain?"

From time to time people would come on stage with some incredible stories about things that had happened to them before their healing.

Spiritual Lip Sync

One day, while a lady from the audience was telling a particularly long and involved story, I noticed that Kathryn's lips were moving. Even though audible words were not coming from her mouth, I was able to read her lips. I could see that Kathryn's lips were simultaneously forming the same words being spoken by the lady, and she only stopped long enough to say, "Yes, and go on, honey."

Only the people who were very near her could see and be aware of this phenomenon. The first time I saw this happen, I just watched in amazement. As a matter of fact, I became so involved in watching Kathryn that I almost lost track of the next person I was supposed to bring to her for an interview.

From that time on, I watched very closely to see whether or not Kathryn repeated this. I noticed that every time she interviewed someone, her lips moved silently, sharing that person's testimony as the Holy Spirit placed in her mind and on her lips the very words that were coming out of that person's mouth.

When Kathryn Kuhlman said that she was the most surprised person in the world as to what happened during a healing and that she had absolutely nothing to do with it, she was not just being humble. She really meant it. She always gave the glory to the Holy Spirit.

Words of Knowledge

One of the most inspiring parts of any Kathryn Kuhlman service was the "words of knowledge" that God would impart to her. I can remember one night, in the early days of my association with her, Kathryn was preaching and she suddenly stopped partway into her sermon and announced, "Somebody is being healed, and you are standing to my left, and it is a back condition."

A young lady standing next to me in the audience startled all of us when she shouted out, "It is me!"

Before this happened, I had stood quietly as this young lady's boyfriend loudly ridiculed Kathryn. Even though I did not dissent, I was like Paul in the Bible who held the coat while the people stoned Steven. As his barbed comments came thick and fast, I kept saying to myself, "You're right. She is a kook."

Much to the shock of her boyfriend, this young lady went up onto the stage. As she stood there trembling, Kathryn asked her, "Are you sure all the pain has gone?"

"Yes," she replied firmly.

Kathryn then fixed her attention on the cynical young man who was wearing a cast on his left leg and said, "God has healed you, too."

His face turned brick red as she added, "Yes, if you stomp down, you will find all of your pain is now gone."

He began to do this and then cried out that he too had been healed.

Kathryn Kuhlman had not touched either of these people, yet both had experienced the supernatural healing of God.

That was one of several things that caused me to become a true believer!

The Jerusalem Press Conference

Kathryn always had an uneasy relationship with the media. Quite often the reporters would attack her flamboyant style, likening it more to Hollywood than to the solemnity of the more staid religion of the midwest where she hailed from.

But she never apologized for her dramatic presentation of the gospel message because she knew that the Holy Spirit was present each time she took the stage, and there were thousands of people who could testify to having received a miracle healing as God had worked through her. She was an expert in the field of the Holy Spirit, and during her day, she was unrivaled.

I was with her during a particularly fraught news conference held in a hotel right on top of the Mount of Olives in East Jerusalem. She was in the capital of Israel to conduct a series of miracle services.

A Jewish reporter, trying to needle Kathryn, asked her pointedly "Why did you Christians come all the way to Jerusalem for your conventions? Why didn't you just remain in America?"

There was a deafening silence in that packed room as every eye focused its attention on Kathryn. I held my breath and awaited her response to this loaded question. The first thing I noticed was her body language. I saw her agitated movement. Kathryn had a way of sticking her tongue out of the corner of her lips and then licking the bottom lip. Her eyes began to flash as if they were beating out a Morse code, and she placed one hand on her hip and pointed the toe of her foot like a ballet dancer.

Then the words came out of her mouth with lightning precision. "Young man," she said fixing her flashing eyes on the reporter and pointing her long, bony finger at him as if she was a maestro conducting a great orchestra, "I will tell you why we are here."

The reporter shifted uncomfortably in his chair as she continued.

"This is God's 'chosen land' and you Jews, whether you like it or not, are God's 'chosen people.' We are here because Christians love your land. We are here on this Mount of Olives because we know that one day it will be split when the King of Glory, the Messiah, Jesus Christ, returns to take up His rightful throne. We're here because He was here at Pentecost when 3,000 people were saved."

Like everyone else, I looked over at this reporter, and I could tell by his look of confused bewilderment that every word from then on from him and the other "scribes" there would be guarded.

My gaze then reverted back to Kathryn. Her face suddenly became soft and filled with compassion for this man. Whenever Kathryn thought that a person was embarrassed by what she had said, she would embrace that person with her arms (with this reporter she just held out her arms and then embraced herself) and would tune her voice to that of a little girl.

"Well, it's just like that, you know," she said softly.

She had made her point and now she wanted to do all she could to not make an enemy of the person who had attacked her. Kathryn knew that by using these tactics she could win over even the most hostile critic, and realized that someday that person might even turn his life over to Jesus Christ. And what better place to do that but in Jerusalem!

The Bodyguard

There is a time when it is hard to trust those who are very loyal to you because they say and do everything that they think you want.

For instance, I remember one time we were in Chicago for a two night crusade, and I watched in horror as Kathryn got confused and instead of exiting at the back, she began to walk in the wrong direction. She was right on the edge of the stage. If she went an inch further, she would fall about 30 feet down into the pit where the band or orchestra was usually situated.

As she stood perched at the side of the stage, I shouted to one of her helpers, "Kathryn's walking the wrong way!"

The man cut me off. "I don't care," he said loudly. "It is the way Miss Kuhlman wants to exit the stage. She knows which direction she wants to go."

Fortunately, she finally realized that she had been going in the wrong direction and halted just before a terrible fall.

I didn't sleep well that night, so the next day I did the unthinkable.

I arrived early and went to Kathryn's dressing room and rapped on the door.

"Cooome in," came the inimitable voice from inside.

I pushed open the door and saw her seated in front of a mirror with bright lights surrounding it like a ribbon.

"Kathryn, I would like to discuss with you last night's meeting and especially your exit," I said.

"Oh yeah, Jimmie," she said as she continued applying the makeup to her face. "What is it?"

I had learned over the years that the way to get Kathryn's attention was to use humor, so I approached my observation in this way by saying, "Well, you see, in my imagination I saw this great lady of faith laying in the band shell with her legs sticking up in the air."

"What do you mean?" she said, continuing with her makeup.

"Kathryn, you don't know it, but as graceful as you are, your legs were leading you to the edge of the platform, and you almost made the 'exit of a lifetime.' "

She laughed and said, in the way that only she could say things, "Oh no, Jimmie! Do you really mean it?"

I nodded my head and smiled. "I did speak to the person who had been accompanying you, but he said you were being 'led by the Spirit.' "

"Oh no, Jimmie," she chuckled. "I was being hauled around by an usher who did not know what he was doing. From now on, I will look at you to see which way I should exit the stage safely. I will be watching for you, and we will start tonight."

But I had forgotten to ask Kathryn what sign she would give me so I would know it was time for me to accompany her from the stage. That night, as the crowds began to swell around her to almost dangerous proportions, I began to panic, not knowing when I should move in and "rescue" her.

Fortunately, she looked at me and gave me what I call a "Holy Ghost wink." I knew at that point that she was ready to exit and so I led her off.

After that time, no matter how big the crowd was on the stage, I always looked for that wink. I helped her off the stage and served as a quasi-official bodyguard for her from then on.

Because of my bodyguard role, Kathryn told me that when we traveled, she wanted me to have a room close to hers so that if she had a problem, she could call me and I could rush to her assistance.

The Intruder

I remember a day during a visit to Israel when the phone in my room rang early in the morning. It was Kathryn on the other end of the line.

"Jimmie," she said urgently. "There's somebody knocking on my door and Maggie [her special assistant] is not here. I don't know what happened to her or where she went. Will you look out of your door and see who is knocking at my door? I am not going to answer it or open it until I know who is out there."

I could hear the noise in the background and commented, "It is a strange knock because it sounds as though they are scratching and trying to get in."

I told Kathryn to hold on and I would check out who was there.

So I looked out and almost collapsed with laughter when I saw the "intruder." It was Maggie!

I ran back in and picked up the receiver. "Kathryn, it is Maggie at your door, and she is trying not to startle you, so she is scratching on the door to avoid waking you suddenly. Everything is all right; she was just trying to gain entrance."

Chapter Nine

A "Word" in the Wings

*I*T WAS TO BE the turning point of my life. I stood once again in the wings of the Shrine Auditorium and watched Kathryn Kuhlman sweep past me and onto the stage, her usual flashing smile lighting up her face and her chiffon gown fluttering behind her, as thousands broke into wild applause, many of whom were waiting for *their* miracle to take place.

After ten extraordinary years with Kathryn Kuhlman, I was beginning to anguish over what I should do. I had been given the possibility of pastoring an African Methodist Episcopal Church in Tampa, Florida, but I needed a "word" from God on what He wanted me to do. I was keenly aware that if I took this church, I would not be able to travel freely with Kathryn as I had been doing.

"Lord," I prayed as I stood in the darkness watching Kathryn at work for her Lord, "please show me what I should do. I need to know!"

"Taking Her Home in Five Years"

It wasn't long before I got the answer that I needed. During that Sunday afternoon service, I was suddenly startled when I heard a still, small voice that I recognized as coming from God, which said clearly, "I am going to take that lady [Kathryn Kuhlman] home to be with Me in five years."

As I listened to this, I broke out into a cold sweat. I had never heard God's voice like this before. I was now aware of the fact that this giant of God was soon to be taken "home." As I looked out at the sea of faces in the Shrine that day, I wondered what they would say if I told them the incredible news that I had just heard.

I realized that I needed a witness to what I had heard from the Lord. The Reverend LeRoy Sanders, pastor of one of the Hollywood churches, was close by in the wings, and I called him and said, "Brother, I need to talk to you."

"Sure, Jimmie," he said in an affable way.

I don't think he realized at that moment the terrible news I was going to give him.

We walked through the cavernous area behind the stage and eventually found a room. When we got inside, I quickly began checking around to make sure that no one else was in the room.

Then I shut the door, and LeRoy asked me, "What is it, Jimmie?"

I took a deep breath and tried to compose myself. "Pastor," I said as my heart thudded unmercifully, "God has just told me that He is going to take Kathryn home in five years. You are the only person I felt close enough to that I could tell."

My words were greeted with a long silence by my friend. It was a cessation of sound that would change the direction of my life. I then shared with him about the possibility of a church. He said nothing.

After the service, I asked Kathryn if I could have a word with her. I knew she was exhausted from another long meeting, but I had to tell her about the offer I had received.

Kathryn listened quietly to me and then said, "Well, Jimmie, you must do what you must do! But, I hope you will still be able to find time to sing for me when you can."

"Of course I will," I told her as I fought hard to staunch the tears in my eyes. "You know that I will!"

"Reverend" McDonald

It wasn't long after this that I was inducted as the senior pastor of this Tampa black church. It was a tremendous difference for me as many in my congregation were on welfare. They were the kind of folk that the "American dream" had bypassed. There was none of the flash and glamour of my life with Kathryn Kuhlman, but I was so happy to be able to minister the Word in my own church.

I still worked with Kathryn whenever I could. I took "red eye specials" to cities all over America to sing at her services, and then would leave straight afterwards to be back at my church as soon as I could.

The Visit

One Saturday night I had a call at my home from Dino Kartsonakis, and I was delighted to hear from him.

"Hi there, my friend," I said amiably. "How are things going?"

"Fine," he said.

"What can I do for you?"

There was a brief silence and then Dino said, "Jimmie, I thought I would tip you off that you will have a special visitor at your church tomorrow morning."

"Not Kathryn," I responded.

"Yes, Kathryn! I wasn't supposed to tell you, but Kathryn told me that she wanted to visit your

Sunday morning service. She knows it's your birthday and she wanted to surprise you. I felt, as a friend, that you ought to be prepared and know she is coming.

"Kathryn doesn't want you to make a fuss."

I thanked Dino for his "tip off" and replaced the phone on its cradle. It was now Saturday night, which meant that I would not have an opportunity to make an announcement to the members of my congregation. I was also aware that they would not have known who she was anyway. I was in an old-line denomination, and those who belonged to it had not seen her broadcasts or attended any of her meetings.

I felt a real excitement that morning as I drove to the church. However, I wasn't sure how my people would react to this flamboyant evangelist.

We had a good congregation that morning and I told one of my officers at the church that a "white lady" would be visiting us.

"When she arrives, I want you to bring her down to the front of the church," I told him.

Then I told the usher, "Wherever I am in the service, please send me a note and let me know that she is here." They realized that white people normally didn't visit our services because we were such a poor congregation.

Our worship time that morning had been typical for a black church, with our choir leading the singing of some powerful choruses and 500 of our people clapping and dancing in the aisles.

But where was Kathryn? I was beginning to get anxious as there was still no sign of her. Then, just before it was time for my sermon, Kathryn made her entrance, and it was not a flamboyant one. She came dressed as an ordinary worshiper. Along with her were Dino, Maggie, and some other friends.

I didn't need that note I had requested because I saw her arrive, and one of my ushers directed her and her entourage to seats at the front of the church.

After she had taken her seat, I tried to explain to the congregation that we had "Kathryn Kuhlman with us." I added, "She is a worldwide evangelist and a person who is being greatly used of God in the world of the supernatural.

"We also have with us, Dino, who is a great concert artist and player of sacred music."

I asked Dino to play something for the congregation. I will always love and appreciate Dino for his graciousness in agreeing to play a piano that was not in tune and did not have the grandiose concert sound he was used to. In fact, this semi-upright piano was in terrible shape with keys missing and a pedal that wasn't working. I am sure that normally he would not have gone anywhere near an instrument as bad as this, but this was a special occasion for him and us.

Dino played like I had never heard him play before. As his fingers flew across the keyboard, he moved the hearts of some very poor people. After the thunderous applause that greeted his performance, I went down the steps to greet Kathryn.

We hugged each other, and then I asked her to please address the church.

Kathryn slowly climbed the steps and then spoke to my congregation.

She said, "The Reverend McDonald, whom I love and affectionately call 'Jimmie,' is a dear servant of God, of whom I am very proud. And you should be proud of him, too."

Calling me "Reverend" was a very wise move on Kathryn's part, for she knew that to call me "Jimmie" in front of my congregation would have been an insult to them. Most black people are very respectful of titles, and I had been sent as "Reverend Dr. J.A. McDonald" by the bishop to my church.

Wearing a conservative, dark outfit, Kathryn had played it straight. There were none of the usual

Kathryn Kuhlman skips and dances. She just stood and leaned over the podium to give my group a low-key greeting.

"I've just come here this morning to worship," she said quietly. "I've chosen your church to worship in, but I want to let you in on a little secret: I have also come to listen to your pastor preach."

With that, she returned to her seat. The applause was deafening. She had not tried to "take over the show" but had come as a member of the congregation, just like the rest.

I do not remember what I preached that morning, but Kathryn said later it was one of the "finest sermons" she had ever heard. But more special than the sermon was the fact that I invited people to come forward for prayer at the end of the service and asked Kathryn to come and pray for the people. This was unheard of in a church like mine.

I saw something that morning that was different from the usual Kathryn Kuhlman meeting. Usually, her services had the right atmosphere, the right organ and piano music, and the right choir, as well as volunteer workers to help with the service. People would come by bus and car with great faith, really expecting the move of God.

But here, I must remind you that this was one of the old-line, staid conservative Methodist churches. I wore a robe and all of the color of the year; I understood the rubrics of the traditional Methodist church.

I had not been there long enough to have transitioned them to the point where they would understand the move of the Spirit. As a matter of fact, some of them were trying to understand why we were raising our hands during worship.

So when Kathryn started to minister, she was moving in uncharted waters.

Many of the people had never been to a charismatic service and didn't know who Kathryn Kuhlman was. They just called her "the white lady."

I saw the power of God move in a powerful way in that service. People were healed, slain in the Spirit, and delivered.

Kathryn had not come prepared with "catchers" and people who understood all that was taking place; and yet the sincerity with which her ministry was done was received by my congregation with graciousness.

Later, as we spoke in my study, I asked her, "Kathryn, if you felt the move of the Spirit, would you come and minister to my congregation some time."

"Of course, Jimmie," she said. "I'd be honored to do so."

Sadly, however, she was never able to come again to my church.

Chapter Ten

The Discordant Note

THE MOST EMOTIONALLY uncomfortable situation for me was during the time that Dino Kartsonakis and Kathryn Kuhlman had their misunderstanding over Dino's romance with a girl named Debby Keener.

I had been vaguely aware of the friction between Dino and Kathryn, but it finally came out one day when Dino and I were in the dressing room at the Shrine Auditorium before one of Kathryn's miracle services. We were getting ready for it and I noticed that Dino was not his usual bright self, but was instead staring blankly at the wall.

"Hey, buddy, what's wrong?" I asked, trying to cheer him up.

Dino sucked in his breath and then turned to look at me. "It's Kathryn," he said in a pained voice.

"What about Kathryn?" I replied.

"I'm beginning to feel like I am trapped," he said sadly. "She is telling me that I must be 'careful about my friends.'"

I replied, "Well, man, that's the price you pay for being in the inner circle."

Dino's Entrance Into the Inner Circle

The path to the relationship between this "Daughter of Destiny" and this incredibly talented pianist began when Dino, then in his late 20s, was invited to play for one of David Wilkerson's monthly super rallies at Melodyland in Anaheim, California, a church that was just a stone's throw from The Magic Kingdom of Disneyland. (David Wilkerson had received worldwide fame through his book, *The Cross and the Switchblade*, which had been released in 1963.) Also appearing at the rally were Pat Boone and Andre Crouch.

After that first meeting, David Wilkerson asked Dino to play the piano as a soloist at his meetings in various cities across the United States.

One night, in the late 1960's, a woman named Ruth Martin came up to Dino after one of these David Wilkerson services and introduced herself.

"You're not only good, but you're too good for these meetings," she said, adding, "You really need to be with someone who can give you a chance to show your talent, a place to spotlight your marvelous playing."

Ruth Martin then mentioned the name of Kathryn Kuhlman whom Dino admitted he had not heard of at that time. Ruth said that she would tell Kathryn about him, and this eventually resulted in this couple being linked together for an extraordinary ministry of praise to the Lord.

Dino described their first meeting in his book, *Dino, Beyond the Glitz and Glamour*. It took place at the Paul Webb Agency in Los Angeles where he had gone to see if they had any bookings for him.

> "As I left the office and walked down the hallway, I saw Ruth Martin and a tall, thin, red-headed woman. Ruth's friend looked like a 1930s fashion model. She was about five-foot eight, and her hair was parted in the middle and curled by finger waves."[4]

Dino remembers Kathryn saying, "So you're Dino," as she dragged out the three words so that they sounded like ten. "Her raspy voice and dramatic gestures and movements increased her intrigue," Dino wrote in his book. "Kathryn lifted her arm, pointed her finger at me and, as if some divine truth had suddenly been revealed to her, repeated, 'You're Dino.' "[5]

This "chance" meeting was the beginning of a seven-year relationship between these two totally different people.

Dino's first assignment was to play on her CBS television show in Hollywood. From then on, Dino became a regular feature of not only her television program, but also her rallies. And every step of the way, Kathryn began to create his image. She staged him and made him appear to be all "glitz and glitter."

"The Greatest Keyboard Artist in the World!"

During each show, Kathryn would stand at center stage and introduce him as if she were heralding the return of some great prophet. "Here's Dino, the greatest keyboard artist in the world!" she would say.

With that, Dino would begin to play, the incandescent chandelier providing the perfect balance between shadows and light, projecting an atmosphere of intimacy to the scene as well as a milieu of both drama and glamour.

The chemistry between the two of them was astonishing. They were, in those early days of the relationship, inseparable, until Debby Keener came on the scene and the whole friendship began to sour.

Dino wrote in his book, "Kathryn helped make me more than a keyboard artist. She possessed an unapproachable mystique and helped establish the same aura about me. I couldn't anticipate the powerful control Kathryn would one day exert in my life."[6]

Kathryn was an extremely private person and did not open up herself to many people, except those in her inner circle, and Dino became one of those honored few.

In order to get some understanding of the powerful emotions that flowed around these two extremely talented people, you have to realize the dynamics that worked between them.

First of all, it is vital for people to separate Kathryn Kuhlman, the world-renowned TV personality, from Dino, the flamboyant musical artist who possessed more than the usual talent, whose creative genius at the piano excelled most of his peers.

Only when you look closely at these two individuals, who despite their abilities had all the human needs of ordinary people, can you then separate the wheat from the chaff in their disagreements.

A Take-Charge Person

I have read books about Kathryn and Dino, as well as tabloid and magazine articles, and heard many discussions about them, but I could always tell that the writers who penned their stories and opinions had not really spent any close-up time around either Kathryn or Dino. If they had spent some time around Kathryn, one of the things they would have discovered right away was that she was a "take-charge" person, and if you did not surrender *all* of yourself to Kathryn, you were not comfortable working for her.

Let me give you an example of this. Several times Kathryn organized a picnic for her beloved choir. She had the food cooked and catered by someone else, but when it came to the feeding of the choir, she put on an apron and then fixed and served the plate of each person there.

Why did she do this? I believe it was because she felt she was filling the void of not having a family of her own and was, for that moment, experiencing the satisfaction of being personally involved in a family-style activity. Her flock was indeed her family, and Dino had become a vital part of it.

Kathryn was also a perfectionist. "I can't help it," she once said. "I want things done as near perfect as possible."

In her office hung a little wooden plaque that her office employees gave her for Christmas. It said, "If it were easy, everybody would be doing it."

In saying all this, I'm not talking about the rights or wrongs of how Kathryn operated, but that's just how she was. She needed to be in charge not because she wanted to be a dictator, but because she genuinely wanted the "best" for the Lord in the ministry that she headed up. It had a lot to do with a deep abiding love and the fact that she really cared about the work that she believed God had raised up. For instance, this kind of posture was in every activity of the church that Kathryn pastored; every service was under her full control, including all of the music.

When Kathryn first met Dino, she saw his great potential and felt that she could make him the "biggest and best" in the world of gospel music and beyond. Whatever doors of opportunity she could find, she would personally try to pry them open for him.

The White House

I remember the occasion when I was invited by Richard Nixon to sing at a special service at the White House following his election as the thirty-seventh President of the United States.

I first met Mr. Nixon in Portland, Oregon, while I was traveling with Billy Graham. Mr. Graham had been agonizing over whether or not he should endorse Richard Nixon as President and called some of his team together to pray with him about it. Mr. Graham had never endorsed a candidate before and finally decided not to endorse Mr. Nixon either.

After we prayed, we were taken to another room to meet with the presidential candidate.

As I stood there, I said, "Mr. Nixon, I would like to call you Mr. President, not just here but at the White House."

I told him that I would also love to sing at the White House someday.

"If I am elected President, Mr. McDonald, you will receive a personal invitation to come and sing at a White House service," he promised.

I had actually forgotten our conversation, so I was shocked and honored when I received the invitation in a White House envelope. As I read it, I realized that I was due to sing at one of the famous Kathryn Kuhlman services at the Shrine at the same time.

So I took the invitation to Kathryn and I explained what had occurred. I thought she would be upset, but instead her face beamed with pride.

"That's wonderful, Jimmie," she exclaimed. "I'd be glad to let you go for an occasion like that."

I thanked her, and as I was walking away she said, "By the way, why don't you take Dino with you as well?"

I rubbed my chin with embarrassment. "I would love to, Kathryn," I said, "but it is coming up so quickly that I don't think there would be enough time for the FBI to conduct the security check on him."

Kathryn's face assumed a quizzical expression, so I explained that the FBI was required to do a far-ranging security check on all people invited to a function at the White House.

"Kathryn, I've already had phone calls from several friends who told me they had received calls from the FBI asking all about me. One of them asked, 'Jimmie, what have you done? The FBI is looking for you.'"

Kathryn was obviously disappointed that Dino could not make it to the White House on this occasion, for she had worked every angle she could to make Dino into a "mega star." She had apparently "adopted" this young man as a surrogate son, and I believe that everything Kathryn did on Dino's behalf has to be filtered through this "motherly love" she had for him.

God had given Kathryn Kuhlman a great big heart for benevolence and, regarding Dino, she was just giving a young man an opportunity to excel in his talent. I believe that she considered his ability as something tremendous that the Holy Spirit could use to bring glory to Jesus Christ.

So, although Dino could not go with me, I had the wonderful privilege of singing at the White House before Richard and Pat Nixon and their many guests.

Creative Genius

I look back on the relationship of Kathryn Kuhlman and Dino from two important vantage points. First of all, Kathryn saw Dino as the son she never had; and secondly, she looked upon him as the highly polished antique that had been sculpted by her own creative genius. It was from those two emotional avenues that Kathryn felt she had the right to attempt to impose some unusual restrictions on Dino.

Let me say here that I do not believe that there was any romantic involvement whatsoever between Dino and Kathryn. She was a strong, motherly woman, bonding with a young man who embraced a strong woman wherever he met such an individual.

It was at that level that the rift came. Kathryn felt that she had the right to "protect" this young creative fledging, and so, from time to time, she offered "motherly advice" on who he should date and be seen with. She did as any mother would by suggesting the "right kind of girl" for him to be involved with.

The problem came when Dino decided he wanted to get married to a certain young lady that Kathryn did not approve of. She came right out and told him, "No, she is not the one for you. She will wreck your ministry."

Some critics have said that Kathryn was jealous, but I believe it was no more than the "taking charge, very caring" side of Kathryn's personality coming out. Her "motherly instinct mind-set" could not understand how you could be loyal to her and still have your own desires and ambitions.

Having worked with some of the most well-known preachers in the world, I must say that whenever you are working with a high profile person in the "supernatural ministry," it is not at all strange for them to not understand anything outside their own ministry.

An Insight From Dino

In his book, Dino revealed his opinion of why Kathryn liked him so much. He said that one day they were talking and Kathryn agreed to tell him about her short-lived marriage to Burroughs Waltrip, a divorcee. It was during this discussion that Dino asked to see a photograph of her ex-husband.

"She walked across the room and opened the bottom drawer of a small dresser. From where I sat, I could see pictures scattered all over the inside. She sorted through them, pulled out one photograph, and brought it to me.

"The moment I saw the photograph, an odd sensation overcame me.

"I stared at the man in the picture, probably taken when he was in his thirties. He had black hair and was dark complexioned like those of us of Mediterranean heritage. And though we didn't look exactly alike, our coloring and eyes were the same. I suddenly wondered if perhaps Kathryn projected some of her feelings for him on me. She had never done anything out of line, but the likeness in the photo arrested me.

"I never asked about him again."[7]

Debby Keener

It appeared that one of the problems Kathryn had with Dino's relationship with Debby Keener was the fact that Debby had admitted to having dated Keith Hefner (brother of the famous Hugh Hefner of *Playboy*). Dino said that Debby had told him about her years away from God and now had said that she again wanted to serve God.

Dino described Debby in his book:

"I thought about her often. Debby Keener is one of those fortunate individuals who seems to meet people effortlessly—so different from me. She also has the ability to put them at ease. As I would see in the days ahead, Debby could walk into a room of strangers and before the evening concluded, she would know most of them. People responded to the same qualities of warmth and friendliness that I liked about her.

"Debby has a compulsion to be the life of the party. I envied that because, frankly, at that time in my life I wanted to party, to have fun, to enjoy being around people my own age. I was tired of being involved in little else aside my uptight work schedule. Debby entered my life just when I needed someone to show me the lighter side of life."[8]

The stress between Kathryn and Dino was also driving Dino into the arms of Debby. He wrote:

"I was conscious of only one thing—Debby Keener was the best thing that had happened to me since I had started to work for Kathryn in 1969.

"Debby was the first girl I felt free to talk with, to really open myself up to, and we enjoyed being together. She encouraged me to talk and to be myself. I admired her playfulness which was such a contrast to everything else around me."[9]

Dino said that she was slowly changing her lifestyle and trying to "live like a Christian." She had been going to church and was starting to get involved in that—although her circle of friends was still "predominantly show-business types."

Dino said that he loved Debby and wanted to marry her, so he proposed to her after seeing her appear in *The Dick Haymes Show*.

She told him across the dinner table, "Yes, I'll marry you."

When the news reached Kathryn, she told Dino, "You're making a big mistake. She isn't for you."

Kathryn repeated to Dino the rumor that Debby had once been a Playboy bunny and had lived in the Playboy mansion. Dino told her that he didn't believe the story, but anyway he said he didn't care about her past. "I love her for who she is now," he declared.

Surprisingly, Kathryn, who based her whole ministry on "miracles," told Dino that "people don't change! If she was that way ten years ago, she's that way today!"

It was around this time that Dino finally realized that no woman would ever meet with Kathryn's approval. "I resented her meddling, and I wonder now if her push to destroy my relationship with Debby didn't actually push me closer to Debby," he said later.

After our conversation in the Shrine in early 1975 when Dino had told me he was feeling trapped, things between Dino and Kathryn sadly continued to go downhill.

In his book, Dino said that when he first hinted that he was leaving, Kathryn became upset. "You think it's easy out there?" she asked. "You think people will come to hear just anybody? Just let me see you go out there and draw five thousand people."

In late February 1975, both of them knew that the end of their relationship had come. Kathryn went ahead and hired another pianist to replace him for the CBS show. After standing and watching the taping, Dino asked Kathryn if he could talk with her.

"Kathryn, I want to get married," he said firmly.

"To the Playboy bunny," she snapped.

Dino attempted to control his temper and told Kathryn that he really loved Debby. But Kathryn was having nothing of it. "Oh, Dino, you will ruin your entire life," she sighed.

The Parting

Dino knew this was the end. As he quit, he leaned over and kissed Kathryn on her cheek. "I want to go out and make my own way," he said. "Good-bye, and thanks for everything."

As he walked away, Kathryn told him, "You're making a terrible, terrible mistake."

In May 1975, Debby Keener and Dino were married in Sacramento. Warren Grant, her former youth pastor and Dino's friend, performed the ceremony. The late crooner Dick Haymes sang "Eternal Love" at the ceremony. Kathryn had been invited to the wedding, but did not come. In fact she even scheduled a service at the Shrine Auditorium for the day of the wedding.

I know how disconsolate this break up made these two people—and sadly, Dino's marriage to Debby eventually ended. He has since married Cheryl McSpadden, whose brother Gary had sung with the Bill Gaither Trio.

But Dino was able to finally express his feelings about Kathryn in an open letter which is carried in the final chapter of this book.

Chapter Eleven

A Ticking Time Bomb

SOMEONE ONCE ASKED me if Kathryn Kuhlman believed in physicians. After all, many reasoned, she was the ultimate "healing evangelist" so why would she need the help of a doctor?

Well, she did. Kathryn had her own physician, but she often neglected to go for a checkup. So the doctor would turn up at one of her meetings, and while in her dressing room, he would tell her, "I have just come to shake your hand."

With that, he would take it firmly and hold her hand by the wrist, tight, for several seconds while he secretly took her pulse. The doctor was only too aware that Kathryn, with her intense schedule, was literally a "ticking time bomb."

Some 20 years before, Kathryn had slipped out of Pittsburgh and gone to see a doctor in Washington, D.C., to have a physical checkup.

"Miss Kuhlman," the doctor had warned her after the checkup, "you have an enlarged heart. You need to slow down."

When he saw the incredulous expression on her face, the doctor threw his arms in the air in frustration.

"Miss Kuhlman, I'm not joking," he insisted. "You have a serious heart condition and if you don't take my advice, you will have a heart attack. Just mark my words."

Kathryn, however, had a way of just ignoring news that she didn't want to hear; so instead of slowing down, she stepped up the pace of her ministry another notch and pressed on with her impossible schedule. She often worked 17-hour days.

During one of her radio programs, Kathryn once said:

"The greatest enemy a human being can take into his life is fear. If you are able to conquer the enemy of fear, you have come a long way toward bringing health to a physical body.

"Life is not built for negative achievement. It's built for positive contribution, outgoing love.

"You can never get rid of your own troubles unless you take upon yourself the troubles of others. When you find yourself oppressed by melancholy, the best way out is to find something you can do for somebody else. When you dig a man out of trouble, the hole which is left is the grave where you bury your own sorrows. Go out each day and do something that nobody but a Christian would do. It won't be long before you'll forget about your own troubles.

"Hard work is about the best medicine I know anything about. The right mental attitude is glorious. Those who sit around waiting for a miracle will seldom find it. You help God from within by giving to others. When you do, miraculously, your fears, doubts, and self-centeredness will vanish."[10]

Jamie Buckingham, in his book *Daughter of Destiny*, recorded an incident told to him by Steve Zelenko, who was producing her radio show. Steve said that after an argument with one of her secretaries, Kathryn walked back into the radio studio in her offices in the Carlton House Hotel in Pittsburgh, her face ashen white.

"Come in here," she told Steve.

Taking his right hand she placed it against her left rib cage.

"I could feel the organ of her heart, beating, trying to force itself out between her ribs," Steve said.

"When I removed my hand I could actually see her heart, pulsating between her ribs—under her dress. It seemed as if it would explode."

Steve said there was an occasion when she was in the radio studio about to make a tape. "I was in the control booth and looked up," he said. "She had disappeared from her desk. I went into the studio and she was stretched out on the wooden floor."

He said that she told him, "Go right ahead. I'm just resting a few minutes."

"I returned to my control booth," Steve said, "but I thought she was dying. I finally came back to the studio and urged her to lie on the sofa. She shook her head and strangest look came over her face."

Steve said Kathryn told him that she would be all right and that in about ten minutes she would be back at her desk ready to go.

"It was as though it had never happened," he said. "But it had."

Kathryn was always living with the possibility of a heart attack. In moments of humor, she would tell the audience at a meeting, "Well, if I have a heart attack, Jimmie will be the cause of it because he always takes the last plane in."

There would be laughter, but she was acutely aware of the weakening heart condition she had. This was the way she was dealing with it.

When she told the story of me "taking the last plane," I would smile. This bit of humor momentarily deflected her mind from the problem that was plaguing her on a day-to-day basis.

Kathryn desperately tried to keep her illness secret from the public, but I knew it would only be matter of time before events would overtake her.

As White As Death

On one day in 1974, Kathryn had gotten sick in Los Angeles and was put on a TWA flight to Pittsburgh. She got off the plane looking as white as death. Being the trouper that she was, Kathryn talked and smiled with people at the barrier who recognized her.

When Maggie Hartner, who had been warned of her condition, picked up her baggage and got her to the car, Kathryn turned to her old friend and gasped, "Get me to a doctor. I'm going to die."

Maggie told her that she wanted to take her straight to the hospital, but Kathryn protested, "No! Not hospitals."

Her secretary knew she could not force Kathryn to do anything she did not want to do, but she also knew that if she did not take urgent action, Kathryn would die. So she drove her directly to the office of a doctor who was aware of her medical history.

He took x-rays and said her lungs were clear but her heart was "radically enlarged." The doctor put her on digitalis, and after one day's rest Kathryn was back to her usual routine.

On another occasion, Kathryn became very sick again. She was staying at the Century Plaza in Los Angeles and was totally exhausted after another CBS taping.

Sue Wilkerson, the wife of "Tink," the used car dealer from Tulsa, had become her confidante and went to her room to see how she was doing. Sue was horrified to discover Kathryn half off her bed, lying face down, too weak to raise her head.

Helping Kathryn onto the bed, Sue told her that she would have to get her to a doctor. Kathryn weakly nodded her head. Her stomach was swollen with fluid and was putting intolerable pressure on her already enlarged heart.

Sue contacted Tink, and he was able to find Dr. Carl Zabia who had helped another friend after a heart attack.

The doctor promised to come right over to the hotel and check Kathryn. He did, and afterwards he called Tink into the hallway.

"She needs immediate hospitalization," he said. "I'll call an ambulance. Give me her records and I'll have them looked over by the time you get her to St. John's Hospital."

With that the doctor called an ambulance from Tink's room. But when Kathryn heard of this, she was extremely upset. Having not spoken a coherent word for some time, Kathryn suddenly sat up in the bed and pushed back the covers.

"I'm not going in any ambulance and don't you mention it again," she said. "Everybody in this hotel will know it and that means the entire world will know it. I'll walk before I go in the ambulance."

Image Is Everything

To most people, this would seem ridiculous, but to Kathryn, "image" was everything. After all, how could the world's most famous healing evangelist be seen leaving in an ambulance?

Rather than waste time arguing, they honored Kathryn's wishes. Tink gave the ambulance driver 40 dollars for the wasted trip and returned to Kathryn's room. Kathryn then began the long, agonizing walk down the hall to the elevator and to Tink's car waiting outside.

Jamie Buckingham described the next few minutes in this way:

"She almost died in the car. In fact, Tink thought she had died. By the time they got her to the hospital she was in and out of consciousness. There was additional confusion at the hospital since Dr. Zabia expected her to arrive by ambulance. It took him almost fifteen minutes to find out where she was, laid out on a stretcher in an emergency room. By that time her blood pressure had dropped far below the point of life, and she was rushed to the cardiac unit where the doctors worked feverishly for almost five hours until she was revived and her vital signs stabilized."[11]

Those of us close to her were asked to "pray like you have never done before," and I, like so many others around the world, asked God to "have Your own way with Kathryn's life."

Amazingly, Kathryn began to make a recovery. Still, the doctors there in California kept pressing Kathryn to let them do a heart catherization. But she refused, saying she had some "personal things" to do first. We discovered later that one of these personal things was to draw up a new will—something that caused much controversy which has already been widely publicized.

When Kathryn was eventually allowed to leave the hospital, she returned to the Century Plaza where she was cared for round-the-clock by nurses, but her life was continuing to ebb away.

Then, surprisingly, Tink felt that Kathryn should be taken home to Fox Chapel, her house on the edge of Pittsburgh. He flew her in his private jet.

After a brief stay, she was carried out of her house to the car and then to the airport to go to Tulsa for urgent heart surgery.

At the hospital, Oral Roberts and Tink Wilkerson gathered in the room where Kathryn was being prepared for surgery. Oral could see that she was dying and laid his hands on her forehead and prayed a brief prayer. With that the two men left the room.

Oral then said, "Whatever you do for Kathryn do it in a hurry. I've never felt death any stronger on a person in all my life."

Then Evelyn Roberts and Sue Wilkerson joined their husbands and returned to the room where Kathryn had been prepared for surgery—Kathryn still lying nearby.

A Jewish doctor who was part of the surgery team then asked Oral, "Why don't we all join hands while you pray for us."

Just a few seconds later, an orderly wheeled Kathryn into the operating room. Kathryn underwent nearly five hours of open heart surgery where the surgeons repaired the mitral valve.

The operation appeared to go well, and it seemed that Kathryn would recover. But then, on the following Friday, Kathryn developed an abdominal obstruction that required further emergency surgery. And, during the subsequent two weeks, the surgeons had to perform three bronchostomies because the size of her heart impeded the drainage from her left lung.

Kathryn again rallied, and we all began to believe that she would recover. I was told to "stand by" for the monthly Shrine services and also a miracle service in Oakland in April.

But it wasn't to be! Kathryn had once again returned to her home near Pittsburgh, and on February 20, 1976, I received a call from one of her aides:

"Jimmie," she said, "Kathryn's gone home to be with the Lord."

I was silent, numb with grief.

I had lost a dear friend—and the world had lost an incredible woman. She may have been imperfect (like all of us), but she was also an instrument that God used to reflect His glory here on earth. I realized that now, in death, she would be able to give Him glory—FACE TO FACE!

Then, something else occurred to me: She had died exactly five years after God had told me that He was going to take her home.

Chapter Twelve

A Final Word With Kathryn

ATHRYN KUHLMAN'S FUNERAL service at the Wee Kirk o' the Heather in Forest Lawn Memorial Park in Glendale, California, seemed totally different than what she had wanted for her "final farewell" from this earth.

I had heard her say, "I want an open casket with all 'the men' singing the praises of the Lord, and I want them to, one by one, give testimony of what they were delivered from, whatever the addiction was. Then, when people ask what Kathryn Kuhlman was about, these men will do the preaching for me."

So, when I arrived at the chapel on that dismal day in Southern California, I was shocked to see a rose-draped closed casket.

"But," I whispered to myself, "this is not how she wanted her home-going."

I looked around the chapel but could not see "the men" that she wanted from her church who had served her and her Lord for so long. The men who were delivered and sang in her choir were not there. The choir members, ushers, workers—none of them were present.

Apparently, Forest Lawn had been given instructions that no one could see the body. They called it a "red tag" funeral, and they had put Kathryn's body on the second floor in a room with one entrance and windows that were locked and barred. None of us who were close to her were allowed to view her body.

The casket was then brought down to the chapel for the service.

As I took my seat with the other handpicked guests, I again looked over at the casket and felt that she had been put in a dark and lowly spot. My eyes measured its width, and I thought it almost seemed too short to hold her.

The question in my mind was, "Why couldn't I see her one last time?" I knew that in that box was an incredible servant whose voice had been vibrant, filled with laughter and pathos; but all I could hear now in that chapel was the hush of the moment, silence broken only by the tears of those there and the sniffing of noses.

Here, in a box, was a woman who used to stand on stage before huge audiences and say, "You knew, he *would* be here! I'm talking about Jimmie McDonald." With that, she would throw up her hands as if it were a signal to the audience to receive me.

Just for a moment, a lump came into my throat. As I allowed my thoughts to take over, the service began and I was invited to come and sing. It was to be the most difficult performance of my life. I was so overcome with grief that I found it hard to breathe.

I also knew that I now stood on the horns of an emotional dilemma. I knew that there was a body in that casket, and I did not have a chance to say goodbye. This was the very person who would always check that the lapel on my tux was straight or free from lint. She would make sure that my bow tie stood straight.

This was going to be the last time I was to be able to sing for her. As I made my way to the front of the chapel, tears now streaking down my face, I felt she would have said, "Jimmie, it's okay to cry, but please go on singing. It's going to be all right. I want to hear you again."

At that moment, I filled my lungs with air, and my vocal chords, which had been constricted with sadness, suddenly became vibrant. I began singing the words of the hymn, "It Is Well With My Soul," with an emotion that I had never felt before.

It Is Well With My Soul

I was singing not only *for* Kathryn Kuhlman, but for a brief moment, I was her voice, clothed in flesh, articulating the words that the body in that box could not speak: "It is well with my soul."

When I sat down, I no longer felt sad, but joyful—joyful that all was well with Kathryn's soul.

Oral Roberts then came to the front and described what happened to him when the news came that Kathryn had died:

> "My whole concern was about the healing ministry. Then I remembered her words and they hit me like thunder claps. 'It is not Kathryn Kuhlman. She cannot heal anybody. It is the work of the Holy Spirit.'

> "Then I saw seven lights and I saw twelve people. I said to God, 'What do the lights mean?' He revealed to me that the light came to people...they were not choosing, they were being chosen. There will be special people raised up out of this. These seven lights will shine out across this land, and in her death her ministry will be greater than in her life."

We all stood to attention as the pall bearers carried her body out. As they passed me, I whispered, "Good-bye, my friend. I'll see you sometime."

She was then buried in a rather anonymous grave with a little headstone that read, "I Believe In Miracles."

I thought she deserved more recognition than this, but then I remembered that it was almost like Moses back in the Bible. God took Moses up to the mountain and showed him where the Israelites were going, but He said "I'm not going to let you go into the promised land." Then, when Moses died, the people never knew where Moses was buried. Probably, the reason for this was because they loved him so much that they would have visited his grave too often, and it would have become a shrine.

I think the reason for the anonymous gravestone, and for locking the gate so that visitors could not come in, was so people would not make a shrine to a woman that God used.

Dino's Letter

When Dino heard of Kathryn's death "from complications from surgery," he decided that he needed to do something to try and explain his deep feelings towards her. He said that his biggest regret was that he wouldn't have the chance to settle things between them.

So he wrote the following open letter to tell the world and Kathryn how he felt. It read:

Dear Kathryn,

This is a letter I've wanted to write to you for a long, long time to say the things I was never able to say to you. I've held this within me, and now I'm determined to express through this letter how much you've meant to me and how much you have influenced my life and ministry. I wanted to see you, to tell you how I felt when you were lying in the hospital. In those dark days, you must have known that you were dying. As I heard medical reports over television, I didn't want to believe it could happen to you.

I was barred from coming to see you at the hospital. I don't know if you knew this. Several of us who truly loved you weren't able to be there at your side. And that's one of the biggest regrets I have. But at last I am getting the opportunity to say these things to you.

Dear Kathryn, you've been a major influence on my life. By your own example, far more than by what you said, you taught me how God can mightily use individuals who totally commit themselves to him.

The other day a man who had been a faithful follower of yours approached me after a concert. 'Dino, I feel that same power and anointing in your music that I have felt in our beloved

Kathryn's life and ministry.' He didn't know it, but he couldn't have said anything more wonderful to me.

Since you died, many Kathryn Kuhlman clones have come on the scene. I've said, as I am sure many of your thousands of followers have said, this can't be. There was only one Kathryn.

Please forgive me for my part in the misunderstanding between us and our sad parting. It has been fourteen years since you left this world and I'm fourteen years older and, I hope, wiser and less rambunctious.

Sometimes, especially when I started getting discouraged, I think of you up there watching me. If you can see what's going on in my life, I hope you're pleased.

And finally, Kathryn, you used to say, "When I see the Lord all I'm going to say is, 'I've tried.'" When I meet God, I also want to look at Him and say, "I've tried."

With love forever,
Your friend,
Dino

Gone But Not Forgotten

Yes, Kathryn is gone but not forgotten. And more importantly, the Holy Spirit that she had introduced to millions is still alive and wants to use those of us who will surrender ourselves to His desire to bring healing and reconciliation to this world.

Are you willing to let Him use you?

I'll let Kathryn tell you her feelings in her own words. This is what she said during one of her radio shows:

"As long as I'm still in this body of flesh, I am susceptible to sickness, disease, sorrow, and heartbreak. It's a body of corruption. It is a mortal body. But one of these days it shall no longer be a vile body. It shall be changed from corruption to incorruption. It shall be changed from mortal to immortal. It shall be raised, not as a vile body, but as a body fashioned like unto His body, the blood of our wonderful Jesus.

"We thrill to the glorious fact that our sins are covered with the blood. But my redemption will never be perfected until that day when that which is now corruption, that which is now mortal, shall be raised in incorruption and immortality. One day I shall stand in His glorious presence with a glorious new body. When the trump of the Lord shall sound and the dead in Christ shall rise first, and those who are still alive shall be caught up to meet Him in the air, so shall I ever be with Him.

"Those who have gone before us are not lost, not separated from us permanently. One of these days I'm going to see Papa again. One of these days I'm going to see Mama again. One of these days I'm going to be with my loved ones.

"I won't exchange that glorious hope for a title deed to all the world. My place in Heaven is prepared. My hope is secure. I'm ready to go—I'll see you on the other side."

I now let Kathryn give the final word:

"Helping people is the most rewarding thing in the whole world. You do not have to be Kathryn Kuhlman to help people. The goal of every Christian, every born-again man and woman, should be helping people. God's children are born to serve. That's what Jesus did. Jesus loved to serve. And if you are a born-again man or woman, you too will feel your responsibility in serving and helping people. It's the most rewarding thing in the world."

Yes, Kathryn would want you to begin your own ministry for Him, our God—Father, Son, and Holy Spirit—in Heaven. Just say *YES* and then act!

Then, maybe *you* will get your miracle!

Endnotes

1. Jamie Buckingham, *Daughter of Destiny* (Plainfield, NJ: Bridge Publishing, 1976), 7.

2. Buckingham, 22.

3. Buckingham, 171.

4. Dino Kartsonakis with Cecil Murphey, *Dino, Beyond the Glitz and Glamour* (Nashville, TN: Thomas Nelson, date), 65.

5. Kartsonakis and Murphey, 66.

6. Kartsonakis and Murphey.

7. Kartsonakis and Murphey, 86.

8. Kartsonakis and Murphey.

9. Kartsonakis and Murphey.

10. Kathryn Kuhlman with Jamie Buckingham, *A Glimpse Into Glory* (Plainfield, NJ: Bridge Publishing, 1983).

11. Buckingham.

If you would like more information, or just wish to contact Reverend McDonald, his mailing address and phone number are:

Jimmie McDonald
P.O. Box 3211
Slidell, Louisiana 70458
(504) 643-1479